Nigell Di

Some of it was Fun

Hugh Falkus

Published by The Medlar Press Limited,
The Grange, Ellesmere, Shropshire.

ISBN 1899 600 280

© 2003 The Estate of Hugh Falkus
Design © The Medlar Press 2003
Illustrations © Scott Adkins 2003

*This book is from
the first edition of which
195 copies are bound
in salmon skin.*

Publisher's Acknowledgements
The Publishers would like to thank Max Hastings
for his kind permission to use copyright material.

Designed and typeset in 11 on 14pt Garamond
by Jonathan Ward-Allen.

Produced in England by The Medlar Press Limited, Ellesmere.

Some of it was Fun

Hugh Falkus

WITH ILLUSTRATIONS BY SCOTT ADKINS

2003
THE MEDLAR PRESS
ELLESMERE

CONTENTS

INTRODUCTION

Hugh Falkus, my shooting and fishing companion[1] for nearly thirty-five years, died in 1996. He was an author/adventurer who to my certain knowledge 'used up' at least six of the nine lives normally the prerogative of felines.

When he was only seventeen years old Falkus bought a very old gaff-rigged sailing boat called *Night Wind* for £5. After doing sundry repairs he sailed her up the channel off the Devonshire coast at night without navigation lights and was very nearly run down by a steamer. The story of his survival as the boat disintegrated and finally sank during the storm that followed is one of the highlights of his first book, *The Stolen Years*.

As soon as he was old enough he joined the Royal Air Force and trained as a fighter pilot. He was stationed at Aldergrove in Northern Ireland and later at Duxford in Cambridgeshire. In the summer of 1940, on the day of his greatest triumph at the controls of a Spitfire - he had shot down three German bombers over France - he was caught unawares by the pilot of an Me-110 Messerschmitt and shot down. He survived the crash but was soon captured and because he was not wearing a uniform under his flying suit, was thought to be a spy and handed over to the Gestapo. His life was saved, with only seconds to spare, by the intervention of a German army officer who rescued him from a firing squad. After many failed attempts, he finally escaped from Oflag VIIC prisoner-of-war camp (at Laufen, close to the Austrian border in eastern Germany) and managed to live rough in the hills for some weeks, before returning to England just before the end of the war.[2]

In May 1951, while making and directing a film called *Shark Island*, he was the sole survivor when the boat carrying the film crew foundered on the Dysaghy rocks near Achill on Ireland's wild Atlantic coastline. Falkus managed to swim to safety.

In this tragedy he lost his wife Diana (editor of *Argosy* magazine), two colleagues and his boatman. As soon as he could, he completed the film in order to help fund the dependants of those who perished. Before resuming his career, in order to exorcise his inner demons, he spent a winter on a small, uninhabited island off the Mayo coast. He writes about this in chapters seven and eight of this book.

Once he had recovered, he continued with his acting, writing and film directing activities and soon met and married airwoman and writer Lady Margaret Vane-Tempest-Stewart. (Theirs was a short-lived marriage as Lady Margaret died prematurely.) Subsequently, he had a long lasting marriage to Kathleen.

He survived another likely drowning in the early 1960s, this time with his friend Frank Plum, when during a squall, their rowing boat overturned in the Irish Sea off Ravenglass on the Cumbrian coast.

All of us who have read English language books on freshwater fishing will be aware that Falkus has written some of the best, but before *Sea Trout Fishing* and *Salmon Fishing* became widely acknowledged as definitive, Hugh had written what is undoubtedly his finest book. *The Stolen Years* was published simultaneously in Britain and the United States but curiously it wasn't until both editions were remaindered that the book slowly but inevitably received full acclaim.

In the Falkus plan, *The Stolen Years* was to have been the first in a trilogy of books covering his whole life, but the vicissitudes of real life caused changes to the plan. Film making and a number of books that assured him some income took priority. He worked on the manuscript for the second book from time to time but did not pursue it according to the original plan. Sadly, books two and three never materialised because Falkus couldn't get the finance - I was with him when he tried - to carry him through the two or so years that he needed to finish the work. Subsequently some of the material intended for the second volume (about his extraordinary life as a pilot before and during the war and his prison camp life) was used as a prologue when a new edition of *The Stolen Years* was published in 1979.

I daresay that readers who greatly enjoyed *The Stolen Years* would have eagerly looked forward to volume two, whereas all those who knew Falkus in his middle life would have looked forward to volume three. This was to be about life at Cragg Cottage in Cumbria where he and Kathleen held court, over a period of thirty years, for some of the rich and famous who came to learn about Spey casting as well as many of the best-known anglers and writers of the day. Cragg Cottage became a kind of 'club' - a meeting place for those whom Falkus called 'Trusties' (as outlined in the preface to the second edition of *Sea Trout Fishing*, 1975).

Hugh Falkus was quite seriously ill during his last years and the drive to record the rich experiences of his extraordinary life seemed to evaporate. Nevertheless, what you are about to read are pieces of the 'lost' manuscript and we are left to judge whether they were intended for the second or third volume. So far as I am concerned, the discovery of this text by Anthony Desbruslais,[3] one of the 'Trusties' referred to above, gives us all the chance to enjoy a previously unpublished selection of Falkus's writing when we thought there would be no more.

Frederick Buller, 2003

1 We co-authored three books - *Falkus and Buller's Freshwater Fishing*; *Successful Angling*; and *Dame Juliana, The Angling Treatyse and its Mysteries*.

2 In the 1970s I introduced Hugh to William Hardy, a wartime captain in the British Army and subsequently the MD of Hardy Bros., the famous fishing tackle makers, when we were all fishing for pike on Loch Lomond. It transpired that William and all the other inmates in the same POW camp had their privileges withdrawn when Falkus assaulted a guard while making his escape.

3 Anthony Desbruslais was Hugh's legal adviser, executor and also a fishing companion in his later years. He came across the manuscript while sorting Hugh's papers and effects following the death of Kathleen Falkus.

I

WEATHERMAN

Most of my life – certainly the majority of my sporting and working hours – has been regulated largely by the times of day-break, moonrise and high water; and, of course, by the weather, particularly when 'taking to the field', wildfowling or wildlife filming. But then, the climate in these islands being what it is, the weather is something that affects all of us. Damp, cold, miserable mornings can create so many aches and pains which, even if they are imaginary, seem real enough at the time. At any rate we have enough to make us feel thoroughly depressed, whereas a fine day lifts the spirit, sometimes even inducing little bursts of hormonal euphoria. So it is not surprising that so much of our day-to-day chance conversation is related to the weather.

So far as today's weather forecasting is concerned, I am not impressed. The traditional gypsy woman with a charcoal stick could do as well it seems to me, despite the modern forecaster's aids of satellite imaging. Presented with convoluted language and much arm-waving, the TV weather forecast has become a 'performance' and I find much of it baffling and irritating.

Over fifty years ago most of the weather details broadcast by the BBC, resulted from readings taken down in pencil on a knee-pad from instruments tied to the wing-struts of an open-cockpit, single-seater Gloster Gauntlet bi-plane fighter, flown at high altitude, as often as not in thick cloud. You may believe it or not as you like, but the ensuing prognostications – prepared by a Cambridge mathematician called Ted, on weather charts, covered with isobars, tacked to a huge sloping desk in a tiny wooden hut on the airfield perimeter – easily surpassed most forecasts on offer today. And I am proud to have contributed to these as a pilot when attached briefly to the Met. Flight in Northern Ireland before the war.

There was no side to Ted, the Cambridge wizard. He was a thoroughly nice chap. An easy-going, amiable, absent-minded intellectual of whom everyone was very fond, but inclined to be rather earnest at times when talking about his isobars, and we couldn't resist taking the mickey.

When he sent up one of his big orange Met. balloons, as he did most days to measure wind-speed and direction at various heights, we were not always as helpful as we might have been. He would inflate the thing from a gas cylinder in front of the hut, and up it would go. And, like the one sent up immediately before it, at about fifty feet it would explode.

"Dear God!" Ted would exclaim. "There goes another. It's ridiculous."

There would be two of us on duty as pilots, and as Ted examined the remains of his shattered balloon, one of us would put another jazz record on the gramophone, to ensure plenty of noise, while the other reloaded the air rifle behind the hut.

Then up would go another balloon . . . and 'thunk' down it would come.

"It's disgraceful!" Ted would complain. "They just don't make these things like they used to."

"No, it's not that, Ted," we would say consolingly. "It's the fifty-foot barrier. There must be something in the atmosphere at that height on certain days in certain weather conditions that simply won't let a balloon go through."

"But I've had no trouble in the past. This must be a weak batch. Don't you think there's a fault in the rubber?"

"No, no, Ted," we'd say. "It's something to do with a band of atmospheric pressure at that height. The balloon will be quite safe at a hundred feet. Bet you."

And I would take a Gauntlet up, trailing one of Ted's balloons and letting it go over the hut at a hundred feet . . . And it would go sailing away.

"There you are, Ted," we'd say. "Told you so. No trouble at that height. It's the fifty-foot barrier that does the damage."

And Ted almost came to believe it. But not quite. He was too astute for that. And in the end, of course, he rumbled us.

Well, childish pleasures I suppose, but at the time it was all great fun. Those carefree, lazy, hot summer days I served in Ireland just prior to the war were some of the happiest of my life. Flying one of the most manœuvrable aerobatic fighters ever made, playing plenty of cricket, whisked off on frequent fly fishing trips by a Commanding Officer who was angling crazy, with riotous parties in the mess most weekends with the chaps from City of Belfast Auxiliary Squadron – a wonderful crowd of sportsmen – life was idyllic and, in later years, never quite to be equalled.

Anyone who could get some fun in those days was wise to grab it. Before the war came and took it all away. As it took most of those Auxiliary pilots, observers, gunners . . . They were a reconnaissance squadron, flying Avro Ansons – pleasant enough aircraft to fly, and splendid for ferrying chaps home for weekend leave, but no sort of machines to go to war in.

When the Gauntlet fighter was superseded as a Met. recorder by the Gladiator, a more powerful aircraft with the luxury of a sliding cockpit-cover, the Gloster Company fitted some of them up with superior meteorological instruments and de-icing gear, and I was fortunate enough to have the task of checking these aircraft at Gloster's airfield near Bristol and flying them back to base. Mike Daunt, the Gloster test pilot, who treated junior Royal Air Force officers like royalty, became a great chum and together with one or two of his cronies and some friendly birds we enjoyed some hilarious parties during my overnight stays at a local inn. In later years his son (of the same name) also became a great mate and has long been one of my rare fishing companions.

* * *

My war started operationally with an air-raid warning on 4th September 1939. Alone, I was ordered up in the same open-cockpit, two-gun Gauntlet fighter (now armed, the only one that was) to defend Belfast shipyards against a long-range, high-level Luftwaffe attack. A photo of that take-off graces the sideboard at Cragg Cottage today: the only surviving picture of my wartime flying. Luckily for me, although not surprisingly considering the distance involved, this attack failed to materialise.

On the way back to base whilst over the Irish Sea, to check what my performance might have been against the Luftwaffe, I amused myself by firing my two guns at an oil-drum drifting on the tide. The result was not encouraging. One gun fired nine rounds, the other seven, before they jammed. Having failed to clear the stoppages – although in painstaking detail I had gone through the customary Vicker's 'four-stoppages' drill – I was forced to land with both belts of ammunition around my neck.

Not long after that, I was posted to East Anglia and spent six months flying daily missions in twin-engined, long-range, short-nosed Blenheim fighters from the Wash to the Thames estuary, protecting east coast food convoys from, mainly, Heinkel attacks.

These simple-sounding operations, were to give me some of the most frightening moments of my life.

First of all there was the aircraft itself. The short-nosed Blenheim was hastily converted from a light bomber to a long range fighter by the simple expedient of replacing its bomb racks with a clamp of six machine guns which, with the original wing gun and one behind fired by a rear-gunner, gave it a total fire-power of eight guns. The only merit in this conversion was the aircraft's range: it could stay airborne much longer than a single-engine fighter – which made it useful for convoy protection. But in truth, it was another of our 1939 aircraft which, like the Anson and the Fairey Battle – to name only two – was quite unsuitable for modern warfare. It offered the pilot little in the way of protection other than a sheet of Perspex, which was terrifying because, make no mistake, those German gunners were very accurate. (A Spitfire pilot in one of our co-squadrons had the tops of both shoulder-straps on his parachute severed by a Heinkel III rear-gunner.)

Another deficiency was diving-speed. The aircraft hadn't been designed for fast-diving fighter tactics. Hard pressed on one occasion amongst snow storms, I tried to outwit a vanishing Heinkel by going into a dive from a half-roll on full throttle. The excessive speed – far above the 'handbook' limits – sprang an oil leak. Suddenly, I was faced with an oil gauge falling to zero, and a moment later the sight of the port airscrew and reduction gear twisting off into space and dropping towards the Norfolk coast. With no hydraulics and only one engine I managed to claw my way back to base, pumped the undercarriage down by hand and landed safely – by good luck finishing up, as it happened, only a few yards from the hangar doors.

So pleased was the squadron Flight Sergeant (a keen fly fisherman) by this fortunate piece of flying that in the workshops during the following week he made me a beautiful little trout landing net – one of the nicest and most appreciated compliments I have ever been paid.

On a second occasion, in similar circumstances, the Blenheim's fuselage on one side stripped off from the cockpit almost to the tail plane, leaving both the gunner and myself exposed to the elements as we yawed and zig-zagged our way home over the North Sea and the East Anglian countryside like an airborne chicken-coop.

But these were minor incidents compared with convoy protection duties. We were nearly always in greater danger from our own ships than from any marauding Heinkels.

Approaching a convoy, and attempting to inspire confidence in the crews, by waggling my wings in friendly greeting, was a signal for every gun in the fleet to open fire. It was the lines of tracer bullets that stretched the nerves, each one seemed to be heading straight up my arse.

The squadron Flight Sergeant, to whom I confided my problem, cut a piece of armour-plating to fit inside the bucket-seat under my parachute. What a splendid man. But, the sense of relief was short-lived on clear days when there was no convenient cloud cover to dart into.

Why did I fly so close? Because those were my orders. "Let them see you," I was told. "Fly over them low down, waggle your wings, it will keep up their morale."

It was *my* morale I was worried about, I would fly along with my sphinctal muscle screwed up tight as a nut.

Repeated complaints to group headquarters resulted at last in a complicated system of signalling by Very lights fired from the aircraft on approaching 'friendly' ships. Each day of the week a different colour code marked 'Top Secret' was issued by some clown at the Admiralty. Thence, in great secrecy, it travelled to the Air Ministry. Then finally, via Fighter Command and Group Headquarters, to the squadron flight-office where by now, usually, we would be sitting in our Mae-Wests and flying-boots playing poker, ready for take-off.

None of this made the slightest difference, of course. On approaching a friendly ship, waving one's wings in exaggerated encouragement followed by the customary display of pyrotechnics, the anti-aircraft firing which, until then, had been sporadic from merchant and naval vessels alike, suddenly intensified to an all-out barrage.

With the cheeks of my bum flattened together like pancakes, I would push the throttles through the gate, haul back on the control column and go scooting up into the clouds where I would remain, until the nautical rush of blood had subsided. On clear days with no convenient cloud cover, I stayed my distance.

Somebody worked out that, on average, by the time it left the Admiralty, the Convoy Identification Colour of the Day was invariably one day wrong for the day in question; two days wrong by the time it had worked its way through the Air Ministry, and perhaps, who knows, even the War Office, to reach the squadron flight-office. On such trifles can one's life depend in wartime, when bullets are cheap. Historically, battles have mostly been won by the side that made fewer mistakes. And perhaps, I should add cynically, issued the most orders. By the law of averages whoever issues the most orders is bound ultimately, to get one right; although . . . as I remember, it is a fact that this never happened to the Convoy Escort Identification Colour of the Day Signal in my squadron.

*   *   *

My companion during most of those Blenheim operations was a Sergeant Rear-Gunner called Smith. I treated him most shamefully. Trained as a single-seater fighter-pilot, I tended to forget I was flying a hybrid with a gunner in the back. Frequently, without appraising him of my intentions, having forgotten he was there, I might suddenly turn the aircraft upside-down or try a series of aerobatics, which the stoic, uncomplaining Smith must have found somewhat disconcerting.

When we got rid of the Blenheims and I was once again on my own in the air, flying a Spitfire, Smith just melted away. I am ashamed to say I do not know where he went or what became of him; a terrible admission of thoughtlessness, but the truth. Reaching back in time for a book like this revives old memories, not all of them congenial.

It is unlikely that Smith will see these words (though not impossible, since he was several years my junior), but if he survived the war, and if he ever happens to read this book, I would like to ease my conscience by saying: "Greetings, Smith! Please forgive me. I was young and silly and insensitive and selfish – and knew not what I did."

* * *

When the squadron transferred to Spitfires and I had a big Rolls engine in front of me I felt safer. Although I still kept that piece of armour-plating under my bum. In the absence of accurate signals, the Navy continued to fire away whenever it had the chance.

This dogged persistence says little for the naval gunners' aircraft identification drill – and still less for the accuracy of their shooting. But in retrospect, considering the continuous cockup of the Colours of the Day, I think I was extremely lucky to avoid giving some bugler the chance of blowing yet another 'Last Post'. . . as indeed I was earlier on, during my training days, when faulty weather forecasting and communication, assisted by my natural silliness, all but did me in.

At the time, we were on an instructional course of fighter air-to-ground firing at a target set up out on the east coast mud flats; but not due on target the next morning, as it happened. Snow storms sweeping the coast had been forecast, so the dawn firing was cancelled.

"Right," I said to myself, "I'll go out on the marshes for the early goose flight." I knew that if the weather forecast was accurate there could be an excellent chance of getting a shot. Bad visibility, I reasoned, would keep the birds low on their flight-line from the distant roosting grounds, and since there was no air firing or bombing practice, the target would provide a splendid screen for me to hide behind. Besides, I had a theory that in bad weather the geese might use it as a landmark on their flight inshore. "What a great chance," I thought, hugging myself. "A chap could wait a lifetime for such an opportunity."

But first, of course, I had to get leave of absence.

"There's no possibility of any firing tomorrow morning is there, sir?" I checked with the Range Controller, a senior Squadron-Leader.

"None at all, Falkus," he said. "It's cancelled. A lot of snow forecast. No flying before lunch. We'll be standing by for the afternoon though, just in case it clears."

"Is it all right, sir, if I slope off early and go wildfowling? I happen to have a gun with me."

"Yes," he said. "Of course you can. Do you good. Do everyone good for that matter. You all spend far too much time in the flight-office lolling about smoking, and playing cards. Do you all the world of good to get some fresh air inside you."

He was a nice chap that Squadron-Leader, if something of a fitness fanatic. But then of course you come across people like that in all walks of life. We even had a few in Fighter Command pre-war, although not many. Looking back, I remember that in those days nearly everybody smoked like autumn bonfires. Silver cigarette cases and lighters with service and squadron crests emblazoned on them were the fashion. The only criticism of tobacco I ever heard was from an amiable, pipe-smoking, medical Wing-Commander who confided his fear that cigarette smoke drifting up the face might ultimately prove damaging to the pilot's eyesight. No one ever mentioned the lungs. As for the other chaps on the firing course getting any fresh air in their lungs, they weren't going to do it wildfowling. I was the only pilot there who had a gun with him.

It was old Puggy Dimmond's twelve bore: the one he had given me years before on the salt marshes by his boat-store near *Seawitch,* the decaying house-boat he lived in. That gun went everywhere with me, I never travelled without it.

Daybreak found me on the salt marsh, sitting on one of the target struts, cradling Puggy Dimmond's gun and listening intently. Any moment now I might hear the sound of flighting geese. What a wonderful chance, I thought, I might never have another like it.

It was bitterly cold and there was an ominous belt of low cloud, but so far the snow had held off, with only the occasional flurry.

And then, suddenly, I heard it. But 'it' wasn't the eagerly anticipated chorus of pink-footed geese, 'it' was the drone of aircraft.

JESUS!

There may have been more frightening moments in my life, but that second of blinding terror is something never to be forgotten. I realised instantly there had been a change of plan: that in the absence of snow storms the air-firing programme had been reconstituted and that in a few seconds a hail of bullets was going to blast me into eternity.

Frantically, I tore off my shooting smock and ran out across the mud flats waving it like a whirling dervish as the first section of aircraft swung low across the marsh.

"Dear God . . . it was my own section!" As one of them said to me later:

"Oh Falky, you stupid bugger! I nearly didn't see you in time. It was only the cloud that kept us so low, otherwise we would have come straight in on attack."

Nemesis awaited me in the form of the Range Controller. Theoretically I suppose he couldn't grizzle too much. After all, he had confirmed the firing was cancelled. But, experience had taught me the impossibility of winning an argument with superior officers over anything they'd declared the day before.

"Oh, Falkus," he said. "You bloody fool! You fucked-up the

firing programme. What the hell were you doing lurking behind the target like that?"

"Well, sir," I said with a light laugh. "With those chaps shooting at it, I thought the target would probably be the safest place."

It was an attempt at humour that went down like an emetic.

"Listen," he said. "You're bloody lucky to be alive. And at this rate, I don't think you will be for much longer."

Well, as things turned out, in this unpredictable and crazy world, he was wrong about that. However lucky and hair-raising the escapes from death that lay ahead of me, I survived the war. Alas, he didn't.

By grotesque misfortune, a stray bomb fell on the local pub one evening and wrote him off. Ironic, when you think that he seldom took a drink. With him went a number of the squadron's ground crew, including the Adjutant and that kindest of fly-casting Flight Sergeants.

I, on whom the odds were shortest, was destined to live the longest. Such is the lottery of life.

II
SUMMER 1940

I awoke to a roar of aircraft engines. Someone was shaking me and shouting. The dispersal-room door hung open. Chaps were running out, buttoning yellow Mae-Wests as they ran.

I pulled on tunic and slacks over my pyjamas and stumbled outside into the half-light. The air was full of noise. There were hurrying figures. Ground crews active by their aircraft; airmen dragging strings of chocks and wheeling the starter-motors clear. On both sides of the dispersal hut, fighters were already taxiing out. Where the hell was my aircraft?

"Over there, sir! Over there!" The Flight Sergeant was tugging at my sleeve and pointing.

I dodged behind a petrol bowser and ran across the airfield perimeter to the Spitfire ticking-over into wind fifty yards away.

My flying helmet hung on the control column where I had left it the night before; parachute ready in the cup of the pilot's seat, a shoulder strap hanging out each side of the opened cockpit. I jumped up on to the port wing feeling the sudden clutch of slipstream ice-cold on my face, then eased myself down into the cockpit, feet automatically finding and testing the rudder-bar. Airmen waited at the wing-tips. I pulled on my flying helmet and jammed parachute straps into the quick-release box.

All clear for take-off. I slammed the hood shut and waved a hand. Chocks slid away and the Spitfire rolled clear of dispersal, the airscrew screaming in fine pitch as she gathered speed. I eased the control column forward and held her steady with rudder. Full throttle. The tail began to lift. A shower of 'golden rain' came streaming back from engine exhaust ports. There was a fast rumble of undercarriage wheels bumping over the grass. Control tower and hangars went past in a blur. Then with a final bump I was airborne and climbing into the dawn sky.

The squadron was circling in formation at a thousand feet. I banked to join up, and we climbed steadily into an empty sunrise. The broad silver ribbon of the Thames estuary fell away astern. At fifteen thousand feet we were over the Channel. A clear, clean summer's morning, with little wisps of cloud and a misty red sun on the rim of the North Sea.

It was very cold. I waggled my toes on the rudder-bar, regretting the flap at take-off. A few minutes more and I should have found my missing flying boots, and had time to grab a cup of tea.

Unexpectedly, a snatch of music came over the R/T. It sounded so incongruous that for a moment everything became detached and unreal: as though I were sitting in a cardboard air-craft suspended above a painted studio sea, with cut-out clouds and a blood-red arc light. I flexed my frozen toes in the elastic-sided leather slippers I was wearing and stared down at the leaden sea. It occurred to me, suddenly, that no aspect of the war would escape the sticky fingers of the film industry. One day, I thought glumly, some director would crucify even the routine job we were doing. It would be charged with emotional clap-trap and larded with the braying background music that destroys every flicker of truth. It amused me to reflect how unlikely it would be if some future film-maker imagined a sit-uation such as the one I was in – when his background music could, for once, be used legitimately.

The music cut out. We droned on through the thin cold air.

Twenty thousand feet below, the French coast stretched mist-ily away into streaks of clouds. A draught was slicing into my right shoulder and my legs were cramped. Never mind, the flight would soon be over. It had all been a flap about nothing. We would be sweeping to the north any minute, and back at base inside half-an-hour. Then, hot tea, a bath and some break-fast.

With dramatic suddenness, little mushroom puffs of black smoke erupted in the sky around me. Instantly, my arse screwed up tight.

A faint *Pom! Pom! Pom! Pom!* More ominous little puffs. We widened formation and began to weave, swinging towards the east. *Pom! Pom! Pom! Pom!* The flak batteries continued to hammer away. Another line of shell bursts spread across the sky. My aircraft rocked violently.

Then I saw the enemy bombers.

They were a mile or two inland at fifteen thousand feet, with a screen of escort fighters above them.

"Bandits! Starboard! Fifty plus!"

The R/T crackled with orders.

"Turning starboard, 'B' Flight. Going in!"

I twisted the gun-button on the control column to 'Fire', banked in a shallow dive and headed straight at the bomber formation.

The flak batteries had stopped firing. German fighters were peeling off to attack. Vapour trails streamed down like ribbons from a maypole. Lines of tracer bullets arced across the sky. A Messerschmitt went flashing past me in a steep dive. There was a knot in my stomach, but this was the moment of excitement that overrides fear and sweeps you on with every nerve stretched tight.

The enemy bombers made no attempt at evasion. I fired at the first head-on . . . and it blew up. The Spitfire shuddered with the blast of the explosion as I swung round in a steep climbing turn. Now the bombers were scattering. One had turned inland just below me and I closed on it from the quarter. I had hardly touched the gun-button when, one after another, the bomber's crew baled out. I stopped firing. White parachutes billowed far beneath. The nose of the doomed aircraft dipped. She went down in a long twisting aileron turn . . . and burst into flames. Dear God! That was two! And I had enough ammunition left to get a third. A third . . . !

I corkscrewed in a tight figure-of-eight and looked hopefully round the sky. It was strangely empty. A feature of air-fighting is the speed with which the sky seems to clear in battle.

Then I saw a lone enemy bomber. It was two or three thousand feet below me, well inland and heading for home. Immediately, I turned and gave chase. It was probably the silliest thing I ever did. We had done our job. The German bomber attack had split up. Alone, with fuel running low, I should have turned back. But there was that single bomber. I had the speed and the all-too-rare advantage of height. And my blood was racing.

The German pilot held his course. My attack must have caught him by surprise. I closed rapidly from above and astern and the moment I opened fire knew I had got him. Bits began to fly off the fuselage. One engine caught fire. Far below, a parachute opened. Then my guns went silent as the last rounds fired. But the bomber was in flames and diving towards the distant patchwork of green and brown and yellow.

Suddenly, something seemed to explode inside my head. There was a crash and a moment of agony. For a second or two a Messerschmitt danced hazily up and down just above and beside me. Instinctively, I dived, trying to concentrate, but for too long everything was a mask of pain. The Spitfire shuddered as more bullets struck. The engine spluttered, picked up, then spluttered again. The gyro compass was spinning; the instrument panel shaking, and mistily out of focus. I had no idea of course or speed – only that my aircraft was out of control and diving.

When my eyes cleared I saw that the oil pressure gauge was reading zero. The engine gave a final cough. There was a frightening silence. Fields and woods were rushing up at me. Dazed,

I tugged the control column. Jerkily, we came out of the dive and began to lose speed. The altimeter showed seven hundred feet. I remember thinking: 'Too low to bale out. *Must* get her down!' There was a big enough field straight ahead, if I could stretch my glide to skim the woods and reach it.

A light flak battery had opened up. Bullets ripped into the wings and fuselage. The cockpit reeked with the acrid stench of hot metal.

'Savage bastards! Can't they see I've got no engine?'

Half crazy with anger and frustration I tried to focus on the blur of green ahead. A row of trees came leaping at me. I pulled the Spitfire up. She ploughed through the branches, shuddered in a stall, then crunched down on her belly in the grass and skidded to a halt.

A machine gun was still firing at me from the wood. By a lucky chance the aircraft was pointing almost directly away from it. I sat hunched in the cockpit as bullets whined overhead and ricocheted off the armour-plating at my back.

The firing stopped. The field was silent and very still. Then, soldiers came running from the woods. I stayed where I was, conscious that by some miracle I was still alive.

They hauled me out of the aircraft at gun point and marched me to a house beside the wood. One side of the house had been sliced away by a tank shell. It was like looking inside someone's skull.

Attempts at questioning me met with no success. The Battery Commander had no English, and I had only a little German. He looked with suspicious eyes at my pyjamas and sent a motor-cyclist to higher authority for an interpreter.

I sat on a stool in what had been the kitchen. It was a sad room and full of ghosts. The former occupants of the house were, I suspected, either dead or herded in some struggling column of refugees. Small personal belongings still littered the mantelpiece. Picture postcards, ornaments, a thimble and cotton. Intimate, tiny things. The bric-a-brac of someone's life. With sudden terrifying insight I understood what it was like to lose everything in an instant. To walk away. To leave one's life behind and start again.

It was happening to me.

The bullet graze on my scalp was the slightest of wounds, but my head throbbed. The sun, which had risen above the trees into a blue and now cloudless sky, blazed through the kitchen window. Another scorching summer's day had begun and already the room was stuffy and hot.

I sat there feeling dazed and numb, tasting the bitterness of my stupidity. I thought of the breakfast I had missed and was never to eat; of the chaps in the squadron, now back at base counting the cost and wondering what had happened. I thought with hopeless longing of the freedom of the clear, cool sky and damned myself for a bloody fool.

But regrets were futile. I began to collect my thoughts. Somehow I had to escape; to get away from these people before the interpreter and his men arrived.

I stared through the kitchen window across a small garden. Woods stretched away beyond the garden's edge, dark and inviting. There seemed to be plenty of ground cover among the trees. The window catch I noticed with growing excitement, was off. I would never have a better chance. An operational flak battery could spare very few men to hunt for escaped prisoners. The sooner I went the better.

The sentry guarding me was a youth of sixteen or seventeen. He seemed a nice enough lad, but I was desperate. I groaned a couple of times and pretended to faint. As anticipated, he stood his rifle in the corner and stepped forwards, peering at me. When he was a yard away I straightened suddenly and hit him at full stretch on the side of the jaw. He grunted and fell on his knees half-stunned against the table. I jerked the window up, jumped through and sprinted for the woods.

Almost at once the shouting started. There must have been a group of soldiers out of sight beyond the house. Even so, I nearly made it. The woods were only twenty or thirty yards away, but just short of the trees an unseen strand of wire flung me headlong into a ditch.

Looking back, I realise it was probably a very lucky fall - as I went down, someone fired a shot and the bullet couldn't have missed by much. But at the time I just lay there in despair cursing.

After that incident they were not so kind.

The interpreter seemed surprised by my pyjamas. I explained patiently that there had not been time for me to dress properly. This was repeated, together with my name, rank and number, over and over again. He remained sceptical, taking the line that officers never flew in their pyjamas.

"I am asking you again. Why are you dressed like this?"

"I admit it's unusual," I said. "But as I've already told you, there was no time. I was late."

"I do not believe you. You have not come from England.

Officers do not fly improperly dressed. Where did you get this uniform?"

"I keep telling you . . ." I said wearily.

"You took off from some landing ground in the south. Where is it? Where did you get the aeroplane? For what purpose were you flying it?"

"Oh, really . . !"

"Why did you try to run away?"

"Because it's my duty."

"*Duty?* Only officers have such a duty. You are not an officer. You are an agent. A spy!"

A warning light began to flash in my brain.

"Rubbish!" I said. "That's utter nonsense!"

The German Major in charge of the interrogation thumped the table and jumped to his feet, screaming at the top of his voice.

"*Silence!* You will be polite to German officers! You are already in serious trouble. You have attacked a German soldier. Do you realise you can be shot?"

I didn't care for the sound of this.

"You can't shoot me," I said, with as much assurance as I could muster. "I'm a Royal Air Force officer. A prisoner-of-war."

This set both of them screaming.

As I discovered later, many German officers and NCOs had a tendency to shout and scream at the slightest provocation. They did it to anyone unable to retaliate – even to each other, if the 'other' was of inferior rank. I suppose it helped to plume up the will. To the onlooker it was comical and rather pathetic. But amusing though it may seem afterwards, to be threatened with a pistol and screamed-at is not funny at the time. Frankly, it is terrifying.

"You are a liar! A shit!" The interpreter was at it again. "Secret agents are not prisoners-of-war. You will be shot, do you understand? You will be shot!"

There was a lot more of this, after which they put me back in the kitchen. This time there were two guards in the room.

I sat on my stool in the corner thinking about it all. That they could seriously believe I was a spy seemed ridiculous. But there was a sick feeling of fear deep down in my stomach.

"What happens next?" I asked the guards as jauntily as I could, in rusty German. "How long am I staying here?"

They grunted and shook their heads.

"It is very bad," said one of them at length. "I am sorry."

He sounded and looked what he probably was – a simple, honest peasant caught up in the machine of war, sorry for a fellow human being in misfortune. His seeming sincerity did nothing to raise my spirits.

"Thank you," I said. "But why are you sorry?"

The soldiers looked at each other.

"They come for you soon," one of them volunteered. "It will not be good for you."

Not very cheerful stuff.

Who 'they' were I could not elicit. My gaolers declined further conversation and my command of German was too poor for me to draw them out, so after a time I gave up trying and just sat in silence with the ghosts of that dusty room, while sunlight gradually slanted across the worn, tiled floor, and lit up the mound of rubble by the stove.

It was mid-afternoon when the 'SS' contingent arrived.

From that point, events took on a dreamlike, or perhaps I should say 'nightmare' unreality. The SS troops wasted no time in living up to their reputation. They kicked me into a car and drove to their base: a farmhouse about fifteen or twenty miles away. There, inside a bare room, the shouting and the punching started. For loutish brutality those troops were in a class of their own. They seemed convinced I was an agent trying to escape from southern France, and wanted a confession to clean up the case.

They worked hard, but I had nothing to confess. And what I told them they did not believe. Afterwards, they dragged me outside into a stone-flagged courtyard and propped me up in the angle of the wall.

On the other side of this old wall was a lovely little stream, just like an English chalk-stream, with beds of cress and ranunculus and grassy banks with a few rushes but many buttercups. A willow tree leaned out over the water from the far side of the stream. Beneath it, a trout was rising.

During the short summer night a sentry stood by to prod me with a bayonet if I moved about or tried to sit down. They gave me nothing to eat or drink.

The following day was another scorcher. From time to time various members of the group came out and screamed abuse. I gathered they were laying on a firing squad at dusk. Not for the first time, judging by the stained flagstones and pock-marked wall. Why they decided to wait so long I shall never know. Wanted to spin out the fun, I suppose.

All through that second, long, blazing summer's day, they

kept me standing by the courtyard wall. I felt utterly alone and helpless and was without any hope at all. I stared at the running water of the stream and closed my mind to everything except that feeding trout. The rugged outdoor nature of my early boyhood had given me exceptional strength and stamina, but it was really the fish under the willow tree that kept me from collapse. In my imagination I tied fly after fly to catch it. I cast over it a thousand times. At dusk, when the soldiers turned out with rifles I hardly noticed them. I was concentrating on the stream. The fish had not risen for some time.

They formed up in a line a dozen yards away. My only memory of the fellow in charge is the size and ugliness of his ears: they stuck out from his cropped head at right-angles – like flaps. He shouted, and the squad sprang to attention. Then for fully a minute he danced up and down in front of me, shouting: "Pig! Swine! English shit!" and other endearments characteristic of the Nazi ritual. When he stopped I told him to 'fuck off'. It was the best I could do.

He gave a howl of rage and slashed at me with his pistol, then swung round screaming orders to his squad.

Dully, almost dispassionately, I thought: 'Well, this is it!' Blood was trickling into my mouth, but I felt no pain. I knew I was going to die and was conscious only of a vague compulsion to make some final gesture of defiance.

All I could think of doing was to turn my back on them.

It was an action neither brave nor cowardly. I had a sudden desperate longing to see that fish rise . . . just once more.

The surface of the stream flashed in the late evening light. Behind me there was a crash of rifle bolts, but miraculously across that shining water ripples were spreading under the willow tree – and somehow I didn't care about anything any longer . . .

"*Halt!*"

The command echoed like a gun-shot. A new voice. A voice of authority. I turned round, dimly aware that I was still alive; that something unexpected had happened. The courtyard was very still. The firing squad stood like a row of images. By the shadows of the barn a motor car had materialised. The passenger's door hung open. 'Big-ears', arms rigid by his sides, was standing to attention in front of a tall, slim, middle-aged army officer immaculate in polished field boots.

There was a rattle of questions and answers. The newcomer looked in my direction and then walked across to me. I was not familiar with German rank badges, but guessed him to be the equivalent of a Major-General.

He said softly, in a perfect English accent: "Who are you?"

I said: "I'm a Royal Air Force officer. They're going to shoot me. They think I'm a spy. It's absolute rubbish."

He nodded. "Get in that car. Be quick!"

I stumbled across and somehow managed to climb in beside the driver. The General got into the back seat and barked an order. As we bumped away along the hard, rutted lane, 'Big-ears' still stood to attention beside his gang of thugs. He looked like a dog that had lost its bone.

We drove on into the thickening twilight.

The tall white chateau stood like a ghost against a background of trees. As we drew up beside the front steps, guards sprang to attention. Inside, troops were billeted everywhere.

The floor of the great entrance hall was littered with equipment. Acknowledging salutes, the General took me up the wide, curving staircase to his room and summoned his ADC.

"Hans!" he called in English. "Come and see what I've found."

He waved a hand. "My temporary headquarters. Rather rough and ready, I'm afraid. Sit on the bed. Have some champagne."

"Thanks," I said, sitting on a pile of army blankets. "Thanks very much."

In retrospect, that evening has an air of total unreality. At the time, too dazed and exhausted to rationalise, I accepted it without surprise – as I had accepted everything that had happened since my capture.

Champagne was produced. The ADC poured it into beer mugs. He was as big as a bear; a huge, grizzled man whose English was almost as good as his commanding officer's. "Sorry," he grinned amiably. "No decent glasses."

"We have to make do with mugs." The General handed me a cigar. "Never mind, it tastes just as good."

I sat on the bed with my mug of champagne and the unlit cigar. My left arm had been stiff and numb since the SS 'interrogation' the previous day. The ADC jumped forward. "Here – allow me . . ."

He struck a match. I held the cigar between my teeth and puffed. No reference was made to my arm, or to the marks on my face.

"Here are some more cigars." The General stuffed half-a-dozen into my tunic breast-pocket. "If you promise you won't set the place on fire I'll give you some matches." He looked hard at me. "Do you promise?"

"Yes," I said.

"Hans – matches."

The ADC pushed a box into my pocket with the cigars.

"Now then," said the General, settling himself comfortably. "First of all, let me tell you that you're a very lucky chap. I heard rumours about a captured pilot and came out to have a look at you." He smiled a tight little smile. "Just in time, it seems!"

"Yes," I said. "My God, yes! I kept telling them who I was, but they wouldn't believe me."

"Listen," said the General. "I don't give a damn who you are, or what your unit is. And I haven't brought you here to find out. I'm just an ordinary soldier, and I'm not going to have British prisoners shot if I can help it. If you'll give me the address of someone in England, I'll get a message through and let them know you're still alive."

This seemed very reasonable. I told him my father's address in Devonshire.

"Good," he said, writing it down. "The message will go through the Red Cross, and it will take time. But he shall know that you are safe. Here, Hans, put this on my desk." He turned back to me. "Tomorrow I will have you sent on to join a prison-of-war column. Tonight you will stay here." He paused, then said very seriously: "I know all about your duty as an officer, but take my advice: don't try to escape from me. You simply do not know how lucky you are." He paused again, then went on rapidly: "I had no authority over those people. I pulled my rank on them, and it worked! But I shall not be able to save you

twice. Those troops . . . they are not the same as us. If they get
their hands on you again you are a dead man!"

The ADC nodded, grinning hugely. "You are very lucky, my
friend. Oho! Damnation – you are lucky!"

The General burst out laughing.

"Hans – fancy thinking he was a spy! Flying in pyjamas. Why
not? All the RAF are mad. It's just what I should expect."

He sloshed some more champagne into my mug.

Hans grinned at me. "Now you are a prisoner-of-war. I was,
myself, for one year a prisoner in the last war. It was not good."

The General laughed again. "He's lucky, Hans. He won't be a
prisoner for as long as that."

And then, suddenly, I got the drift. I understood the champagne and cigars; the easy informality with a captured enemy
pilot; the general back-slapping and bonhomie. They thought
the war was as good as over.

When I told them it was only just starting they roared with
laughter.

"My word, you have some spirit. France lost. The Channel
ports occupied. And you say the war is *starting!* Hans – here is
spirit for you."

"Peace will be made any day now," said the ADC wagging his
head, regretfully it seemed. "England cannot go on fighting
with the German army just across the Channel. If she does not
make peace," he went on soberly, clenching a huge fist, "we
shall invade!"

"That will not be necessary, Hans." The General spoke with
quiet conviction. "There will be peace within a month. And I'm
glad. I've had enough fighting. Besides – I shouldn't like to

invade England. I'm very fond of the place. Spent a lot of time over there."

My head was throbbing. The room seemed to be swaying in a mist. But this patronage was more than I could stand.

"You're talking nonsense!" I said hotly. "You haven't a hope in hell of invading England!"

The General regarded me with an amused blue eye.

"You really believe that? . . . Hans – he really does believe it. It says much for their spirit. It also says much for their propaganda!"

He pushed forward a plate of bread and sausage.

"Ach – who cares? Here, eat some food, young man, and forget about the war – it is nearly over. Have some more champagne . . ."

He kept his word, that German officer who saved my life. His message to the effect that I was still alive reached my home, via the Portuguese Red Cross, nearly two years later. Memory holds a vague impression of his thin, intelligent face, perfect manners and aristocratic air of absolute authority – but not, alas, his name. I have often wondered what happened to him, and whether he survived the war he thought would be over in the summer of 1940.

I hope so.

My life after that was a succession of prison camps in northeast Germany, Poland and Silesia. Bed-boards and straw. Meagre food. Dusty compounds, with machine-gun guarded, floodlit, barbed-wire entanglements; shooting 'incidents'; confusion; patriotic faith; German hatred; repression and frustration. There were interminable journeys between camps in crowded cattle-trucks; periods of solitary confinement for 'anti-German activities'; a long forced march through the Silesian snow in front of the advancing Russian army . . . One lived in hope, the occasional food parcel, as much humour as one could muster, letters from home – and dreams.

Escape? I worked on thirteen tunnels, the longest was over three hundred and forty feet, but they were all comparative failures. In the end a fellow fighter pilot and I cut our way through the wire. It got me home just a fortnight before the war in Europe ended.

At the demobilisation centre they issued me with a suit of clothes, a pair of shoes, a raincoat, a hat and a railway warrant. I gave the suit and shoes to an airman, left the raincoat in a pub, and threw the hat out of the carriage window.

And that was that.

But you cannot so easily rid yourself of memories. I shall never forget the crash of rifle bolts in a shadowy French court-yard, with its little stream shining in the dusk, and then as though in a dream the ripples of a rising fish.

Looking back across a lifetime, it seems that for me this fish has always been a symbol of deliverance. My turning away to watch that trout for the last time undoubtedly delayed those SS thugs for the vital seconds that saved me from a very sudden death. And so often the fish, in one way or another, has kept at bay the increasing horror and madness of the post-war years.

III
THE VALLEY

At sunrise, not long back from the war, I was perched on a broken dry-stone wall beside a beautiful little salmon and sea trout river listening to the distant background music of a mewing buzzard and watching the sky catch fire behind Scawfell.

I had never seen anything quite so lovely. Painted forever on my memory is that particular picture of the valley, with its tree-lined river and the fells beyond. Ribbons of mist clinging to the water gradually dispersed and disappeared as sunlight spread above the hills. Shaking with the ripples of a leaping salmon, the surface of the pool below me reflected undulating ribs of red and yellow flame. In bankside hazel bushes a willow warbler sang. High overhead two ravens croaked as they flew across the valley from a distant crag. No noise of traffic or sirens or shouting voices, only some chimes from a faraway clock and a constant soft chuckle of water at the weir. It was all so natural, so quiet, so peaceful, so unspoilt.

Then, as the sun climbed higher, lifting the shadow from the mountains, two things happened that had a profound influence on my life. From a fellside farmhouse, a young girl appeared and started to feed some chickens; while, further along the fell, slanting sunlight flashed suddenly on the windows of a small grey cottage I had not noticed before. Instantly, the thought occurred to me that any sportsman who found himself living in that cottage, with a stretch of water on the enchanted river I was fishing, would be the luckiest man alive.

Little did I dream that twelve years later, in the autumn of 1957, the chicken girl and I would get married and live in that little cottage ever after . . .

* * *

Looking across the valley from Cragg Cottage (where I am writing this), I can see the track the Romans used nearly two thousand years ago. They marched up and down the valley between a fort on the flank of Hardknott Mountain at the top and the fort of Clanoventa on the estuary near Ravenglass at the bottom – a natural haven that once harboured the Roman fleet.

Hardknott Fort, eight hundred feet above sea level is one of the most remarkable Roman remains in Britain. For me it has great atmosphere. It was built between AD 120 and 130; to control the Roman road over the tortuous 1 in 3 pass between the forts of Ambleside and Ravenglass – part of a strengthening of the hinterland of Hadrian's Wall. Its name was Mediobogdum – 'the fort in the middle of the bend'. (The bend in the river.) 'An enchanted fortress in the air,' one nineteenth century writer described it. From the building inscription, found in 1964, we know that the fort was manned by the fourth cohort of Dalmatians – an auxiliary unit, five hundred strong, from what was recently called Yugoslavia. The stone would have been set above the main gateway. It was made mostly of local rock, but the red sandstone blocks round each of the four gateways must have been trundled up by ox-cart from the coast, because there is no local red sandstone. The main gateway led up towards the administrative blocks, the granaries, and the CO's quarters.

A feature of Hardknott is the old Roman parade ground – an artificially levelled patch of about three acres, two hundred yards north-east of the fort. On one side of it are the remains of a man-made ramp. This mound was the tribunal or saluting base from which the commanding officer took the parade. Perhaps once an Emperor of Rome stood there, and addressed his Dalmatian cohorts. Outside the north gate is a precipice overlooking the river. From it is a wonderful view of the mountains that has inspired many writers, Wordsworth among them:

> *Wheeling aloft the Bird of Rome invokes*
> *Departed ages, and still sheds anew*
> *Loose fragments of wild wailing, that bestrew*
> *The clouds and thrill the chambers of the rocks,*
> *And into silence hush the timorous flocks*
> *That, calmly couching while the nightly dew*

Moistened each fleece, beneath the twinkling stars
Slept amid that lone camp on Hardknott's Height
Whose guardians bent the knee to Jove and Mars.

To us, it is a scene of romantic beauty. But to the soldiers of southern Europe, Hardknott in winter must have been a dreadful posting. How many men, I wonder, stood on that rock and dreamed of home? A fatigue party down-valley to the coast must have been a welcome relief from the rigours of life in Hardknott Fort.

As the raven flies, it's about ten miles to the estuary mouth and we get an idea of what the valley must have looked like centuries ago as we travel down towards the old Roman fort at Ravenglass.

Once these Cumbrian fell-sides were dense forests – mostly oak and birch – the haunt of deer, wolves, boars, eagles, kites, pine-martens. Gradually the forests were cleared to promote grazing land for sheep, and iron smelters cut down the remaining trees for charcoal. Sheep prevented the regeneration of trees and bit by bit the bracken took over. But of course, our countryside has always been in a state of change. And for some of us a skyline of bare fells is more pleasing to the eye than a line of factory chimneys!

During recent years where oak trees once stood, trees of another sort have been planted in small patches, mainly larch and spruce, and I have no quarrel with this restrained and careful planting. Various species of wildlife are returning: blackcock, for example. They put on a fine show when they're competing for courtship territories in the spring but to see all that you would have to be up on the crag and hidden before daybreak.

The roe deer is another creature which takes advantage of new plantations and they've more than trebled their numbers here in recent years; so have some of the passerines: spotted fly-catchers, goldcrests and tree creepers among others. Apart from the change of trees these local fell tops can't have altered much since the days when the Bronze-Age Britons lived here. They had a settlement up on Latterbarrow next to Raven crag behind the cottage and probably used the crag as a lookout point. You can see a long way from there on a clear day. To the south are the Welsh hills; to the west the Isle of Man; to the north the Solway and the Scottish hills, and eastwards straight up the valley lies Scawfell mountain and Hardknott.

On either hand, dry-stone walls stretch for mile after mile into the wilderness – reminders of the enclosure acts of two hundred years ago when fifty thousand acres of Cumbrian fells were sealed off by the Georgian squirearchy – a legalised rape of the common rights.

Perched high above the valley is Devoke Water, surely the most beautiful of all the lakes. Its lonely shores are reputedly haunted by the great white sow of Eskdale – perhaps the ghost of the sow of *Alba longa*, the white pig whose litter represented the seven hills of Rome. And you can believe that if you want to. The brown trout in the lake were said to come originally from a special strain introduced centuries ago by the monks of Furness Abbey. Whatever the truth of that, they were inclined to be small and hard to catch, but very good to eat. Nowadays, the lake is stocked with rainbows.

At the bottom of the valley, where the river becomes tidal, stands Muncaster Castle, built eight hundred years ago. From the castle terrace, looking up towards Scawfell, is a view described by Ruskin as 'The gateway to Paradise' and I won't contradict him. The oldest part of the castle was once a pele tower that somehow escaped the ravages of civil war. It has certainly seen some strange happenings.

Among its more illustrious visitors was Henry VI, during the Wars of the Roses. He took refuge at Muncaster while on the run after losing the Battle of Hexham.

Visible from a window in what was once the royal bedroom, is a tower built to commemorate the spot where the wandering King was found by two estate shepherds. They brought him to the castle, where the owner, Sir John Pennington, hid him. In return, the King gave Pennington a bowl – known as 'The Luck of Muncaster'. It looks rather like a custard bowl, but I imagine it must be of great value.

In spite of all this excitement, one of the remarkable characters the castle can boast is Tom Skelton, or Tom Fool, the last Jester of Muncaster – said to have been known to Shakespeare, and to be the man from whom the term 'Tom Foolery' was derived. He certainly had a bizarre sense of humour. A full-length painting of him displays his last will and testament. In it he says:

> And when I'm buried, then my friends may drink
> But each man pay for himself – that's best, I think.

What *they* thought about it isn't on record.

But Tom was more than a miser. Among the Pennington family, who for centuries owned the castle, was young Heloisa Pennington – whose portrait hangs in the great hall. Although betrothed to a local squire, she had the misfortune to fall in love with an estate carpenter called Richard the Joiner. The squire, who suspected there was some hanky-panky going on, gave Tom Fool the wink to keep an eye on things.

Not a man for half measures, Tom did better than that. He arranged for Richard the Joiner to get into the castle at dead of night for a clandestine meeting with his lady love in an upstairs chamber of the main tower. Then, when simple Richard was sitting in the chamber, waiting, Tom (who had been lurking in a secret passage) pounced on him with an axe and lopped his head off.

The passage from which Tom Fool is supposed to have sprung out and clobbered the unfortunate carpenter, is in the wall of the original pele tower, which – as I know, for I have seen it – is immensely thick. A spiral staircase leads down through the wall to ground level. This is the route Tom probably took when disposing of the body.

It is said that on a wild winter's night you can hear poor Heloisa wailing for her lost love, and see the ghost of the unlucky joiner shuffling about. Presumably looking for his head.

* * *

The Roman fort at Ravenglass was called Clanoventa - meaning 'The Station on the Shore'. According to Tacitus it was the scene of bloody mutiny when a garrison of auxiliary troops butchered their Roman officers, and seized three ships. One of the later regiments that manned it was a cohort of Morinians – from the Pas de Calais.

Right beside the site of the fort is a salmon trap that has been in use for hundreds of years, and regrettably still is. Probably the Romans, too, caught salmon on the same spot. Certainly, it was here that their ships would have been drawn up.

Just outside the ruins of the fort at Ravenglass is a unique piece of Roman two-storey building. The highest standing above ground in Britain. It was the soldier's bath-house and club. Here, the troops would relax and gossip and play dice. A niche in the wall may once have held an image of the Goddess of Fortune.

For nineteen centuries those stones have stood where the Romans placed them. And if you, too, stand here at twilight as I have done, it is not difficult to recapture the sense of a haunted place – and imagine the ghosts of Roman soldiers moving in the dusk.

The ruins of the Roman fort at Ravenglass bring our little travelogue from Hardknott to an end. Here, curling round between two great sweeps of sand dunes, that once sheltered the Roman fleet, the river becomes an estuary – and the estuary becomes the sea.

* * *

It was here on the Ravenglass sand dunes that Professor Niko Tinbergen and I made some of our television films about animal behaviour.

For many years in a research camp among the dunes, Tinbergen and his group of Oxford post-graduate zoologists studied the behaviour of animals in their natural habitat: gulls, crows, terns, oystercatchers, ringed plovers, foxes, hedgehogs, natterjacks, vipers and many more, all of which found their way into films such as *The Gull Watchers; The Sign Readers; The Specialist* and *The Beachcombers.* Now our work is just a piece of history. Niko Tinbergen who, with Konrad Lorenz, was one of the first to make a scientific study of animal behaviour, is dead. His students have long dispersed, and become well-known in their own fields of research. All that remains of their camp, half-swamped by sand among the marram grass, is a small heap of stones.

When I wasn't filming I used to spend a lot of my spare time fishing off the coast at Ravenglass. Whatever its mood, the sea is never safe. To fish successfully, you need skill and knowledge, and a nose for weather. From seawards, the mountains hang behind the sand dunes like a painted back-cloth. But this is a bad coast. Shoal water and rocky outcrops. A sudden shift of wind and you can be in trouble. Bruises are easily come by when the boat is rolling almost on her beam ends, and you're braced against the pitch of the sea – trying to haul the net.

"There is an inherent spirit for hunting in human nature as scarce any inhibitions can restrain," said Gilbert White, and there is no doubt in my mind that he was right. I believe that, basically, all men are hunters, and need to satisfy their hunting instinct. And to do so, some hunt for money, or acclaim, or power. But I just hunt for food. To live largely on what we hunted ourselves was a part of my upbringing, and despite the pseudo sophistication of modern British society, I have never lost the fierce feeling of independence engendered by my attempts at self-sufficiency.

This may seem a primitive philosophy. But it is, I maintain, as valid as any among the vagaries of a primitive and contradictory life that nobody understands. I know that when my work was hung-up and I found myself dragged down into the dark undertow of despair, there was no better therapy than a day or two at sea. I would come in physically exhausted, mentally refreshed, supremely happy.

*   *   *

In the lane at the bottom of the garden my two labradors look happy enough, sitting on a little mound, guarding their territory. Just inside the open door of the garden shed, swallows are feeding their young birds – just as they were in my film *Self Portrait of a Happy Man,* when our white cat, Puddy, was up on the roof of the shed trying to catch them. Twenty-two years old when he died and, although not as nimble as he used to be, still a great hunter right up to the end. A highly skilled bat-catcher, he would sit up on the cottage roof behind a chimney stack and grab them as they flew past. Although, I suppose, this was accidental (I don't believe for a moment that Puddy could have worked it out), the chimney stack acted as a radar screen. He was, indeed, 'invisible' to them, and if one fluttered past close enough . . . Pow! As soon as he'd snatched one he would bring it down via a convenient damson tree and into the kitchen to play with, and usually it would escape and fly up and hang upside down from a ledge on the wall just above my chair.

For a time I knew nothing about Puddy's bat-catching pro-clivities. I would come in at daybreak after a night's sea trout fishing and find those bats hanging up and wonder how on earth they got there – until, one morning I found a pair of ears lying on the floor! Then the penny dropped. The following night I went out into the garden to watch how he did it, and saw him in the moonlight up on the roof, hiding behind the chimney pot like a little white ghost.

* * *

'England,' wrote John Buchan, 'is full of patches which the tides of modernity have somehow missed.'

From the cottage there's a magnificent view right up the val-ley to Scawfell. Nothing I've ever seen in Britain, or Europe, for that matter, looks finer than this 'patch' at summer daybreak with the sky alight behind the mountains and the river a ribbon of mist, glowing pink in the early sunshine.

From my window, at dawn, I've watched a fox kill lambs in the field not a dozen yards away (it had gone long before I could get outside through the kitchen door). I hammered on the window and the fox looked up as cool as you like, then trot-ted calmly off with a lamb in its mouth.

The fox is often thought of as being only a carnivorous beast and, of course, it is mainly a meat-eater; but it also eats a lot of fruit and vegetables, grass, apples, plums, blackberries. The fact is, the fox will eat almost anything that's available, including most types of carrion. When a bird or mammal dies of natural causes the remains aren't wasted. Besides being killers, foxes are scavengers and they can smell carcasses from a long way off.

But because of hygiene may of these remains are buried or destroyed and nature is not allowed to take its course. This is rather hard on the fox. Difficult then, I feel, to blame him when he turns to lambs or game birds and poultry.

From the same window I've watched a buzzard catching moles when they move along their surface tunnels, in the early morning; the barn owl, hunting at dusk, and the tawny owl at all times of the day. Often the raven, and sparrowhawk, and occasionally a golden eagle.

Nearly every day if there is no disturbance, a peregrine sits on the telegraph pole outside my bedroom window. When I've been working late at night and have a lie-in next morning I can sit in bed and watch it. There aren't many people who can do that with a peregrine. As regular as a striking clock it comes between nine-thirty and ten. A bird of habit, the peregrine. Slipping sideways off its perch, its speed at take-off is astonishing. Blink your eyes and you miss it. One minute it's there, the next it has vanished. Then, as you look away you hear a 'hacking' cry, and there it is again – just like a photographic slide show.

The valley resembles a wildlife hotel, catering for a host of visitors that come and go according to the seasons, as well as a lot of residents – including that familiar bird of the motorways, the kestrel. Gerard Manley Hopkins' lines in praise of it are arguably the finest ever written about any animal:

> *I caught this morning morning's minion, kingdom of daylight's*
> *dauphin, dapple-dawn-drawn Falcon,*

in his riding
Of the rolling level underneath him steady air . . .
My heart in hiding
Stirred for a bird, - the achieve of, the mastery of the thing!

Our local kestrel used to live in the fork of a Scotch pine on a knoll behind the cottage. For years it nested there, almost next door to the nest of a carrion crow. Rather odd, really. I wouldn't have thought it possible. But there they were.

Close by is a little beck that flows from the Latterbarrow Crag through the group of pine trees. Herons fish it for eels. Sometimes, when a heron has had a meal it flies up and tries to settle in the crow's tree and the crow, which is fiercely territorial, zooms out like a fighter-plane and drives it away. I've seen it happen several times, and we even filmed it for one of my TV wildlife programmes. The heron doesn't bother much, just flaps off and fishes the beck higher up.

I wonder what Hopkins made of the buzzard? It's a majestic bird and he must have studied it often enough, if only during the days of his Welsh posting, but, so far as I know, he never wrote about it. The one I watch seems to have the cottage right in the middle of its territory. He's often mobbed by the cottage colony of rooks. They hate him, as they hate all short-necked birds-of-prey. But seemingly unworried, he shrugs them off and glides to a distant fence pole, or his favourite perch in the upper branches of an ash tree, from which he swoops down to snatch the moles from their surface runs.

About fifty rooks live just outside the kitchen window. A lot of people don't care to have them close to a house because of the noise they make. But I like rooks. I like their raucous sounds especially when the young birds are being fed. What difficult birds they are to observe. So crafty. All the corvids are difficult to watch. But the rooks, up there in the tree-tops, so many pairs of eyes, all so sharp, really are a challenge. I know, I made a film about them.

Behind the cottage is Raven Crag. An impressive hunk of rock, and aptly named. Ravens have nested there ever since I've known it. They're magnificent fliers. Aerobatics were the abiding pleasure of my fighter pilot days, but, I'll give them best any time. I've watched them give some wonderful displays in the up-draught on the flanks of Raven Crag. Three ravens in tight 'V' formation, zooming down in a near vertical dive, and then breaking away in a 'plume-of-feathers' like black fireworks as they swoop upwards – just as we did in Spitfires all those years ago – then forming up again, and going through almost every variation of flight you can think of. Wonderful performers. To my mind, the best of all. I shall probably be accused of being anthropomorphic, but no one will ever convince me that those birds aren't enjoying themselves.

There are roe deer in the clumps of bog myrtle in the moss down towards the river. All along the river bank are the buck's fraying-stocks – juniper and hazel bushes mostly, with the stems peeled clean of bark by the buck's antlers, where he's rubbed up and down to leave his scent as a signal to other bucks. And across the valley is the fragile delight of the willow warbler, followed by the whitethroat, blackcap, garden warbler and, of course, the cuckoo - when I hear its call I know the spring has really come.

As the year lengthens, the valley becomes alight with wild flowers. I used to have great fun trying to find new species. The names have always fascinated me. The spring flowers are over, and now we have the dog-rose, honeysuckle and wild iris. Meadowsweet, that grows here in profusion. Marsh bird's foot trefoil – whoever thought of that name? The spotted marsh orchid, amongst the bog myrtle where the pheasants nest. The hawkbit with its gorgeous tone of yellow. Love-in-a-mist, campion, ragged robin, herb robert, bird's-eye, bryony and the ubiquitous foxglove – to name only a few. Then the insectivorous species – one in particular.

Up on the moorland in the sphagnum moss amongst the bog myrtle and cotton grass and beautiful little clumps of water forget-me-nots, is one of our most astonishing plants, the sundew. It is so tiny and yet so dramatic. Of all plants it is one of the most beautiful and the most deadly. It lives on the flesh of insects which it traps with its leaves. Each sundew leaf is festooned with tentacles that end in gorgeously-coloured droplets of highly viscous fluid. This substance is very attractive to insects and very dangerous. In one of the programmes I worked on with Oxford Scientific Films – those wizards of natural history film-making – we filmed the sundew with time-lapse photography, showing a leaf in action, curling round a trapped mosquito to catch it and eat it. Fantastic!

It is easy to be cynical, to take nature for granted, but the older I grow, the greater my sense of wonderment. I marvel at the drama taking place within that tiny world. One footstep would blot it all out.

* * *

Two of my favourite flowers are the harebell and the wild thyme. But for me as a fisherman there's one species that has a very special significance, the beautiful little betony – the 'sea trout fisherman's flower' I call it, for it always seems to bloom when the fish come up from the sea.

To search the river for the early arrivals is always exciting. It's one of our great events of the year. And there they are - pale shadows hovering. The first sea trout of the summer! It's a wonderful sight – and it has its own particular magic. Yesterday, this pool was empty. Now, suddenly, these fish have materialised. Even though the river is low, they left the sea last night and ran upstream under cover of darkness.

I watch them with a sense of timelessness. Surviving innumerable dangers, sea trout and salmon have been breeding in this river, going to sea and returning to spawn, for thousands of years. And will do for thousands of years to come – if we give them a chance. Not so simple as it sounds. Half the rivers of Europe are dead. Ruined by pollution and/or acidity. But although its runs of fish are only a fraction of what they were, this little river is still crystal clear – and the fish it holds are still gloriously wild. Sea trout are some of the shyest fish that swim, with the lightning-quick reactions of the wildest animal. A careless flicker of movement from me on the river bank – and alarm begins to spread throughout the shoal. And, suddenly, the stage is empty. But they'll still be in the pool tonight, and my hunting instincts are ablaze. I long to hook one of them.

There are lots of ways of hooking sea trout. But by far the most exciting is with a fly at dusk. It was Arthur Ransome who said that to catch a fish on a fly you have tied yourself is much more satisfying than catching a fish on a fly that someone else has tied, because it better satisfied the fisherman's instinctive desire to depend on himself alone in this voluntary contest with nature. And you know, he was absolutely right. The fish I catch tonight – if I catch any – will mean all the more to me because I have tied the fly I hope to catch them on.

At dusk, the air is thick with the scent of honeysuckle and bog myrtle. The two most evocative scents I know. I can never smell either without being reminded of a dusk-shadowed pool at twilight, with bats flickering about the tree-tops, and owls hooting from the darkening woods, and the sound of water at the weir – and down towards the pool tail the splash of a rising fish . . . That is pure enchantment.

I arrive in the hush of late evening when the sun is sinking behind the fells and the valley is in shadow. In the fading light, I ford the river through fast, shallow water, leading towards the pool where, earlier, I saw the shoal of sea trout lying.

'Parting day' – Thomas Gray wrote – 'leaves the world to darkness and to me.' But of course it doesn't! Evening brings its own solitude, but you are never really alone on a river bank. A raven on its way to roost circles overhead, its flight feathers magnificently spread, like the fingers of two outstretched hands. A barn owl flaps silently across the water meadows, and I remember those evocative lines of Meredith's:

> *Lovely are the curves of the white owl sweeping*
> *Wavy in the dusk, lit by one large star.*

as I stand watching my fellow hunter swoop over the shadowy fields, with Venus brilliant in the west.

In the slanting light, a cock pheasant struts towards the bog myrtle in a marshy hollow – from which a roe deer has emerged to start foraging for its evening meal. The valley is very quiet. There is only the sound of the river – and coming across the water meadows the chimes of a distant clock. And soon, out come the other creatures of darkness that keep us company at the waterside – the badger – and the fox – all the animals that are just going to start their night's hunting.

You don't often see many of these nocturnal animals. One or two owls; a night jar, perhaps; a roe deer that comes down to the river at dusk. And, if you are very lucky, perhaps a badger. There's one that comes down from the woods and spends part of the summer there. It lives in an old rabbit hole, and hunts for food along the river banks at night. It crosses the river by the same footbridge that the dogs and I sometimes use, and digs a lavatory at each end of the bridge – handy for whichever side of the river it happens to be hunting on.

One season it took a fancy to my little fishing shelter. More than once on arriving to fish at dusk. I've gone to the shelter to hang up my tackle bag – and found the badger in possession. What pleasure. It adds another dimension to the sport of angling.

But even though many of these nocturnal animals are unseen, it is not difficult to detect their presence. In wild places, things really do go bump in the night – although most of the sounds are very faint. Bushes swish. There is a rattle of shingle; a whistle; a plop. A rabbit thumps; roe deer bark; a fox screams from the fellside . . . And always there is the soft background of running water at the weir.

There is nothing, *nothing* in the whole sport of fishing so enchanting as a sea trout spate river in the drowsy dusk of a warm summer evening. Downstream where the river shines in the fading light, a myriad of gnats dance in a shimmering cloud. An early bat flickers above the trees. A faint wind flutters the leaves. The fascination of a darkening river deepens, and where the current chuckles against mossy stones beneath overhanging branches, all is shadowy and mysterious.

An owl hoots from the fellside. For a while there is no other sound except the murmur of the river. And then, suddenly, the splash of a sea trout in the pool below. That could be a running fish. On the other hand, it could be lying there, restless and perhaps ready to take. Well – I shall find out . . .

To start fishing too soon in such low, clear water is a great mistake. But it's dark enough now. The sun has long dipped behind the fells, and local colour has disappeared. As I go into the river, Arcturus, the night fisherman's star, is shaking in the water at my feet.

Everything after nightfall is done by touch. I am filled with tense anticipation, expecting at every cast to feel the sudden draw on the line as a fish takes the fly – my first sea trout of the season. I can no longer see the pitch of the line, but I can feel the movement of the fly sometimes when I draw in line as it swings across the pool.

To fish well at night demands absolute concentration. Even the 'kewick' of an owl can be distracting. But there is nothing more disruptive than the sound of the human voice – which is why my two labradors are the ideal fishing companions; they don't chatter!

Again, the line sings in the air and the fly swings round the tail of the pool . . . Suddenly, there is a long, slow tug – then the splash of a leaping fish . . . Yes! I've got him!

But the fierce elation I feel when I hook a fish changes when I start to play it. To outwit my prey; to induce it to take the fly – is everything. After that I want to kill it as quickly as possible.

This one's a good fish all right . . . Sea trout fight like tigers . . . so easy to lose them when they leap . . . But he's nearly ready to land . . . If he'll only stay on while I get the net under him . . . Now's the time when they come off . . . just as you draw them into the shallows . . . But not this one!

I hold the fish in my hands and gaze at its beauty. The sea-silver of its side shines in the moonlight. I have a feeling of great achievement – and yet, a curious regret. A strange dichotomy that many hunters experience; a part of their affinity with wildlife I suppose, a respect for their quarry. But when all that is said, there is no better fish for the table than a fresh-run sea trout. It'll taste wonderfully well with a lettuce-and-cucumber salad.

The short, dramatic midsummer night is over all too soon. Fishing stops at daybreak and with two tired dogs, and a bag of sea trout, I make my way up the fellside . . .

Back at the cottage, I drink coffee and whisky and watch the sunlight spreading behind the mountains. The river is shrouded in mist. From far in the distance comes a curlew's haunting cry, and high above the cottage meadow a lark is singing.

Ever since the war I have relied on my earnings as a free-lance, in whatever capacity, and needless to say, like all self-employed hacks I couldn't enjoy such freedom and independence if I didn't work hard. As usual the 'in' tray on my desk is full, so I have a lot of paper work to do before going to bed. But after a night's fishing there is always time to stand and stare – to breathe the morning freshness, and catch the beauty of the sunrise . . .

* * *

During the halcyon days of high summer the river usually drops to its lowest level and the fish move into the deepest parts of the pools. Grey, unmoving shadows, each dark spot on their flanks standing out with vivid clarity, so transparent is the water, so still are the fish lying. Some are tucked away underneath the bank, others lie motionless under canopies of trailing alder roots or the leafy shade of overhanging branches. From many a crevice in the rocks the tip of nose or tail protrudes, the fish's presence often unsuspected until a few tell-tale bubbles wobble to the surface and break in the sunlight.

When one considers the dangers they have faced, their arrival represents a tremendous achievement. From the moment the eggs were laid in the clear, shallow water of some feeder stream, these fish have been vulnerable to an army of predators; brown trout, eels, gulls, herons, cormorants, mergansers, kingfishers, seals, all take their share of salmon and sea trout at various stages of development. 'The secret splendour of the brooks' Tennyson called the kingfisher, but it feeds avidly on fry. There are few kingfishers in the valley and who would deny such a gorgeous little bird a meal? Unlike the mergansers and goosanders. They, too, are handsome birds, but murderers of salmon and sea trout parr. The heron has a stab at anything it can lift with its long dagger beak, but it's not a serious threat since it feeds mainly on eels and frogs. Otters are a rare threat these days and I for one have never begrudged them their fish. The seals that wait outside the estuary are entirely another matter, they account for huge losses. And then, of course, there are the netsmen: the drifters taking a monstrous toll of the adult fish heading for their parent rivers. In the rivers themselves the fish are targets for poaching gangs that can strip a pool in a single night with nets, poison or explosives. And finally, of course, there are the anglers, people like me, but the threat I pose is not very serious because I fish mainly for the pot. There is no better fish for the table than a fresh-run sea trout, straight from salt-water, a fish like a bar of silver with the tide-lices still on it. And if you've never tasted one you are only half alive.

* * *

No mention of summer would be complete without a brief reference to the cricket as we played it years ago. The village wicket could have been described as 'sporting', but although there were many better pitches there were few, I fancy, set in such beautiful surroundings. And, if you think that local cricket was all boots and braces, let me just disabuse you.

There was, for example the last match I remember playing in the valley, which was for a special trophy against a touring side from Liverpool. We had no truck in those days with the silly idea of limited overs and played always to the clock. Having won the toss, the opposition promised to bat until tea time. A feat they accomplished through fielding an unusual number of players. At tea they were 140 for 19. Batting with a more conventional side, we had scored 130 for 8 when stumps were drawn – dead on opening time at seven o'clock. But being already in possession of the trophy, the 'ashes' were, so to speak, retained in perpetuity. Dictated by tradition, when the pavilion flag came down, the beer was pulled.

Apropos of the number of players fielded, whoever came up with the crazy notion that a game of cricket or football has to be played with eleven a side? You can have a jolly good afternoon at either game with six or sixteen players a side, and more or less, I often have had.

* * *

So soon the colours of the countryside are changing to those of autumn. Every year, it seems, summer's lease is all too short. The sun is losing its strength, there's a chill in the air, winter threatens and the last of the swallows are going. Many have gone already but the later broods have lingered until now.

Now, in this season of mellow fruitfulness, Kathleen gathers the berries and wild fruit used for the jellies that complement the hares, rabbits, game and wildfowl I shoot in winter. We take our share of rowan before the thrushes and starlings strip the lot. The summer migrants that came into the valley last spring are setting off on their long flight to southern Europe and beyond; soon our winter migrants from the far north, the redwings and fieldfares, will be moving in.

The dogs are fascinated when they see either of us up a ladder collecting berries, seeming to think it strange that anyone should climb to nowhere. And you may think I write too much in this book about my dogs; but you see, they play such a large and happy part in my life. I know there are people who hate dogs, but I feel there must be a great chunk of living that dog haters understand absolutely nothing about.

I've always thought it better to keep more than one dog at a time, if it's practicable, because of their origin; a pack, in which they would automatically enjoy the satisfaction of mutual grooming. Sometimes at Cragg we've had three labradors, but usually it's been two. Our present two, for example, are Drake and Leo. Before that it was Baron and Diddy. And before that, Prince and Stinky Wow-Wow.

Stinky Wow-Wow . . . there was a real character for you. Rather a comical name, but then he was rather a comical dog. Prince was just mad keen and quite straightforward, but Stinky, no, he was a great individualist. Both were good retrievers but Stinky preferred to do his retrieving, when possible, underwater. He would hunt all the way along the river bank looking for stones that attracted his attention, then he'd duck right down to the bottom and come up with a big round stone, which he could just get into his mouth, and come waddling up the bank with it. Even today there are mounds of stones that he'd fished out all along the river bank. He was a compulsive retriever and if you left him alone he would spend hours at it summer or winter.

In his later years he was an old gentleman of great presence.

Rather deaf, he took life very much at his own pace, but he used to love the race he had with Prince whenever we went down to the river.

We usually started the race from a gateway called a 'heck' in the field leading to the water. A heck is very simple; just two great big slabs of slate with holes cut in them. When you want to use it as a gateway you put a framework of poles across from side to side. It's very primitive but very practical. The one I am talking about, has some initials cut in it and the date, '1819', just four years after the Battle of Waterloo. But I expect the slabs have been there for many years longer than that. It would be nice to think they'll be there in many years to come, because there aren't many gateways like that about nowadays.

When we had the race Stinky would be given a tremendous lead because he was going rather lame, but, even so, Prince would nearly always win. Not that the result mattered much. Stinky Wow-Wow wasn't really competitive. I was the finishing line, of course, and they would come charging at me. Then on a summer day, we would all roll about in the long, flower-scented grass among clumps of rushes while I made a great fuss of them. It was very simple pleasure, but the dogs enjoyed it, and so did I.

I used to think this sort of dog play was important, and I still do. I feel sure that if we want happy dogs, we should contrive situations where we can behave as 'top dog' and make a fuss of them. After all, their ancestors were wolves, animals that live in groups, and now they're domesticated we must give them the dominance, the affection, the mutual contact they would get in the natural state from other members of the pack and for which, even now they are domesticated, they must feel an instinctive need.

We filmed a dog race sequence for my valley programme; and, judging by their letters, the viewers loved it. Mind you, I don't do so much rolling about these days, my knees aren't what they used to be, and needless to say there isn't, nor ever was, much racing done in the driving rain and sleet of winter, when an east wind like 'a whetted knife' comes whining from the frozen snow-covered slopes of Scawfell. But we do our best.

* * *

When the weather begins to harden, in comes another migrant welcomed by few, hated by many, the pigeon. Fleeing the Eastern winter, pigeons come to Britain in their millions and join the already huge flocks of home-bred birds. They do a great amount of damage to farm crops. If you get the chance, just examine the contents of a pigeon's crop; the result of one day's feeding. It is staggering. But they make wonderful sporting targets. Shooting them is hit or miss as they flight over the trees, and the dogs make sure that nothing is lost.

Shooting makes little or no impression on their numbers. But, although under-rated, pigeons are very good to eat in a roast or in a pie, and for anyone who really appreciates good food the pigeon and game pâté Kathleen makes is right out of this world.

With dogs to feed, very little that is eatable ever gets thrown away. Of course despite all our efforts we're nothing like self-sufficient at the cottage, but we don't do too badly. There are few people in this country, I fancy, who enjoy better food than ours.

Besides fish fresh from the river and the sea, and game from our shooting, as well as wild-fowl from the marshes, there is an occasional sheep from the fell, vegetables from the garden and Kathleen's bread from the oven, the best I've ever tasted.

When my gun comes out the dogs are in their element. In the film *Self-Portrait* . . . I showed Prince, one of my labradors, doing the job he'd been trained to do and doing it supremely well. As one might expect, his sire was Sandringham Sidney, the Queen's famous field trial champion, which is why I called him Prince. Subsequently, all my dogs have been from his strain.

As the days shorten, the migrants that came into the valley last spring gather preparatory to their long flight south – the warblers and swallows and swifts to sunny Spain and Africa – and, before long, in come the winter migrants – the redwings and fieldfares that have spent the summer overseas in Scandinavia, Siberia and Iceland.

Mists hang over the water meadows. In the river, leaves are drifting downstream towards the sea and going with them, during the dark nights of September and October, are the adult eels, beginning the long journey home after years of life in fresh water. The eels that came up long ago as tiny elvers are making their way from tarns and lakes and rivers and little becks and ditches, sometimes even travelling overland on the first stage of their migration back to the Sargasso Sea.

Eels spawn only once. Having spent seven to twelve or more years in fresh water depending on their sex, the adults set off on their long journey home to reproduce and die. And whilst the catadromous eels glide seaward they pass the returning anadromous salmon that are swimming upstream from the sea, two mysterious and fascinating species whose life-cycles act in reverse. Of these two silent migrations moving in the darkness, one has just come thousands of miles from the distant Atlantic, the other has thousands of miles to go, both for the same purpose: to procreate.

Like the ships in Longfellow's poem they are fish that pass in the night. 'Then darkness again and a silence . . . '

*   *   *

Another early winter or, if you like, late autumn visitor to the valley is the woodcock, perhaps the most fascinating and mysterious of all our game birds. Certainly, to my eyes, the most beautiful. It comes, mostly from Scandinavia, arriving usually at the time of the 'hunter's moon' in November. But, in addition to the migrant birds there is also a small resident population. The male bird's strange habit of 'roding' or 'roading' – flying round and round at dusk just above tree-top height on a roughly triangular course, making a low croaking sound followed by a 'skreak' – is well known.

The shape of their flight path may vary, but it seems to have exact turning points. One bird that regularly roded close to the cottage, always turned precisely over the ruined barn below the garden; this would take place always in the breeding season between early March and August – the woodcock having two broods.

As to the woodcock's gastronomic value, people are divided.

I enjoy it enormously, but my wife, Kathleen, can't stand it. Some gun dogs won't eat it, and refuse to retrieve it. Fortunately, Drake, my present labrador has no such qualms.

On shooting days, the woodcock is a wonderful and highly prized target, lurking usually in birch coppice, at the foot of holly bushes and thick cover. It flickers through the trees with an owl-like swerving flight that makes it a notoriously difficult bird to shoot. And, I confess to having fired at and missed more than I have hit.

There is only a scattering of woodcock in the valley at any one time, certainly on our shoot, so we don't get much practice at shooting them. But apart from this, I sometimes wonder why I've never been much of a shot at this tantalising little bird, thinking, that perhaps my aim is inhibited by something deep-down in the sub-conscious; after all, it really is such a beautiful creature. At least, that's the excuse I make for myself. Although I don't believe it.

The woodcock is something of a *rara avis* in English literature. It finds a mention in 'The Blue Carbuncle,' a story from *The Adventures of Sherlock Holmes,* appearing on Mrs Hudson's menu at 221A Baker Street. But, since he seems to have thought that a single woodcock could feed two active men, I don't think Sir Arthur Conan Doyle was very familiar with the species.

Holmes's case concerns the search for a goose that has swallowed a precious stone. As he explains to Doctor Watson: "The question for us now to solve, is the sequence of events leading from a rifled jewel-case at one end, to the crop of a goose in the Tottenham Court Road at the other."

Watson expresses his interest and announces his intention of returning that evening, "To see the solution of so tangled a business."

"Very glad to see you," says Holmes. "I dine at seven. There is a woodcock, I believe. By the way, in view of recent occurrences, perhaps I ought to ask Mrs Hudson to examine its crop."

Later, before dinner, after a visitor has come and gone, leaving him with an important clue, Holmes asks: "Are you hungry?" "Not particularly," replies Watson.

"Then I suggest that we turn our dinner into a supper, and follow up this clue while it is still hot."

"By all means," agrees Watson. And off they go.

But by the time our heroes return to Baker Street, after spending several hours on a bitter evening rushing round Holburn on a goose chase, Watson must have been feeling pretty peckish.

"If you have the goodness to touch the bell, Doctor," says Holmes airily, "we will begin another investigation in which also a bird will be the chief feature."

There the story ends. But one may imagine that to the now ravenous Watson the sight of that diminutive bird sitting alone on its dish must have come as something of a shock.

There is another point, which exposes a crack in the great detective's immaculate reputation. Like that of the snipe and other waders, the alimentary tract of the woodcock contains no crop. Gizzard, yes. Crop no. Holmes's proposed instruction to Mrs Hudson to examine its crop was, therefore, a nonsense, and Doctor Watson's medical training in digestive systems must surely have enabled him to spot his friend's mistake. What a golden opportunity to avenge himself of those intellectual slights he had so often suffered over the years: "Well, Holmes," I hear him say, brushing the last of the woodcock off his whiskers and sniggering at his pun. "I'm afraid in this case, my dear fellow, you have come a bit of a cropper!"

*   *   *

Mid-winter, the valley is silent. The migrant birds have long since gone. A raven croaks high overhead, a cock pheasant crows in the darkening woods. There is the distant echo of a hunting horn high in the fells: the local huntsman heading homeward with his hounds.

The lower reaches of the river, fringed with ice, flow under bare branches. On beds of gravel washed by a current of clean water the salmon and sea trout are collecting to spawn, as they have done for thousands of years – the first step towards a future generation. I look at them with a feeling of helplessness. Ours is fast becoming the age of the artificial: nature trails, heritage centres and man-made lakes with hand-fed stew-pond fish. But, these fish I am watching are gloriously wild, as wild as the river that flows around them. They are part of a scene we cannot afford to lose. As Ruskin said: 'Landscape is part of the nation's wealth.' And clean water is an essential part of that landscape.

At the river mouth the miles of sand dunes lie silent and deserted, most of the boats are laid up for winter. The mudflats hold only a scattering of waders common to every estuary. A few herring gulls scavenge along the tide line; high overhead some wigeon packs whistle in toward the saltings, a solitary oyster-catcher comes piping from his mussel beds and flickers along the shore.

Across the long sweep of dunes there is only the sound of the wind and a distant sea. Until another spring, they are left to the sheep and the rabbits – and the lonely fox.

IV

MIGRANTS

Sea trout and salmon are migrants, of course. And as I have
already intimated it is the valley visitors, whether they stay for
a few weeks or months, or pass quickly through, that for me
exert such a powerful fascination.

Sometimes, in February, I hear the wild music of Bewick's
swans heading up the valley from the estuary. They have been
resting on a sand bank for a few hours after flying from Ireland
where they spent the winter. Now, they sweep past the cottage
on the next stage of their long journey to faraway Siberian
breeding grounds.

There is magic, too, in the stories of the migrant warblers and
redstarts and whitethroats that nest in and around the garden.

According to the *Oxford English Dictionary,* a garden is 'an enclosed piece of ground devoted to the cultivation of flowers, fruit or vegetables.' So I suppose the enclosed patch beside Cragg Cottage does qualify for such a grand title – but only just. Most of it is wilderness – apart from its little lawns in front, which we keep mown.

I call them 'lawns' in defiance of those cretinous social workers in libraries and departments of education who comb through the split-hairs of popular literature seeking words and expressions that are not 'politically correct'.

'Lawns', for example, are considered 'elitist', on the grounds that only rich and privileged people have them. I wonder what they would make of Cragg Cottage lawns, which are about four yards square; and, for that matter, what they would make of Cragg Cottage as an elite residence. It all makes me fear for our national sanity. Somehow one expects such idiocy in America, whence it sprang. But not in the 'land fit for heroes!' Come to that, I wonder what they will make of this book? With a bit of luck they might burn it or sentence me to death – but I'm afraid that's expecting too much.

Mind you, we like our garden the way it is. So do all the creatures that share it with us, and there are plenty of them. If the surrounding valley is a splendid five-star hotel, then our garden is simply a small but congenial suite in that hotel.

What would the world be

wrote Gerard Manley Hopkins,

> *once bereft of wet and of wildness? Let them be left,*
> *O let them be left, wildness and wet;*
> *Long live the weeds and the wilderness yet.*

I think Hopkins would have approved of our garden. And possibly Ruskin, too. He certainly waxed lyrical about the view up-valley to Scawfell. Manuring parts of it over the years with honest farmyard muck has resulted in rich and fertile soil that produces a luxuriant crop of wild flowers and weeds, and these – aided by the ivy-covered dry-stone walls, brambles, nettles (where the lovely red admiral lays its eggs), damson and apple trees and some currant bushes – offer a variety of little animals a high standard of living.

The mixture of wildness and cultivation is very satisfying. Wild flowers are no less beautiful than cultivated ones; indeed, more so to me (as they were to Ruskin) for they are more natural, and I like natural things. But we do have a variety of daffodils in spring, after the crocuses and snowdrops have gone. In summer the cottage walls are a mass of roses, with a number of annuals growing among the weeds – mostly in pots and old fish boxes – and clumps of columbines and a herb patch of thyme, sage, fennel, parsley, mint and dill. And even outside the greenhouse, due to the weird alchemy commonly called 'green fingers', my wife, Kathleen, manages to produce some vegetables – despite the rabbits!

They come and they go, those rabbits. Early one spring, a doe dug a stop at the top of the garden among the snowdrops, where once a pheasant had nested, and I hadn't the heart to shift her.

A 'stop', by the way, is a hole dug by the doe, some distance from the main burrow, where she brings up her young. Fascinating to watch; we could see it all from the bathroom window. At daybreak, there she would be at the opened mouth of the stop, feeding the baby rabbits. Then, after covering up, she would disappear like a wraith and not return until sunset.

One of my labradors – who enjoyed bird nesting and, in consequence, was forbidden the garden during the summer – found the rabbit stop in the end and dug it out. He had been very curious about being banned from the garden so early in the season and one day, when I wasn't looking, jumped the wall. But he was too late; by then the young rabbits had departed. Surprisingly and fortunately they didn't return, so that most of Kathleen's lettuces survived.

But the runner beans and peas are doing badly now, what with the wet weather – and the mice. Times have changed since Puddy went. Puddy was a wonder cat, quite the best hunter cat I've ever known. Strange, really, considering his lack of camouflage, for he was the purist white. But he made up for that by super stealth. When he died there was a noticeable increase in wildlife – rabbits and mice in particular and garden birds, of course. The bats, too, have had a better time of it.

I used to watch Puddy's antics from the window of the garden shed. He was very frightened of strange noises and I remember seeing him stalk an old cock pheasant in the lane. When he was two or three yards away, the pheasant – which until then had been unconcernedly pecking at seeds – suddenly turned round and gave a tremendous squawk. Puddy fled like a streak of white paint.

But I see some interesting things from my study window, too. If you keep still, windows make good observation hides, and mine is no exception. It looks out on the lower half of the garden and across the valley. From my desk I can watch a lot of nesting activity, and sometimes roe deer when they come up from the bog myrtle to nibble bramble tips by the dry-stone wall where, occasionally, the buzzard sits, and the secretive little garden warbler builds. Fox, stoat, weasel, hedgehog, red squirrel, mole, all pass through and leave evidence of their passing. And, in their seasons, migrant birds on passage look in for a rest or a meal of weed seeds before continuing their journeys.

One afternoon, a pair of strange-looking little birds joined some goldfinches that were snatching a feed of thistle seeds just outside my window. Not knowing what they were, I quickly looked them up. Arctic redpolls – very rare vagrants, according to the book.

Next day, a friend came to stay – an ornithologist of repute. When I told him what I had seen, he shook his head in lofty scepticism and nothing I said would convince him. And then, came the kind of coincidence that happens perhaps once in a lifetime. While we were sitting there arguing, those Arctic redpolls reappeared and, for a few glorious seconds, hopped about on the window sill not three feet from his popping eyes.

Oh, noble thistle! At that moment I felt absurdly proud of our garden.

*   *   *

Animal migration seems miraculous. If only because of the enormous distances involved. We can only marvel at the wheatears from Africa, ensconced in old rabbit burrows on the fellside behind the cottage. Each bird weighs no more than an ounce. These have wintered in Central Africa, which they reached by flying south. But wheatears that nest in Alaska take a westerly route over Asia and the Middle East. Those that set out from Greenland may not touch land again before Spain – a flight of two thousand miles over the Atlantic!

Then we have what I call the 'bird of Britain'. Surely no birds are so loved as the swallows.

Flying at a speed of between thirty and forty miles an hour, they cover six thousand miles from South Africa – a round trip of over twelve thousand miles – at odds of three to one against. Yet unfailingly, every spring, two tiny scraps of beauty arrive to take up residence in the garden shed. But what exactly do we mean by 'spring', and when does it start?

When the hounds of spring are on winter's traces
The mother of months in meadow or plain
Fills the shadows and windy places
With lisp of leaves and ripple of rain . . .

When, I wonder, did Swinburn think that winter finished and spring began? After all, even the time of the vernal equinox, traditionally the spring's first day, varies between 20th and 22nd March.

Contrary to general belief, there is no 'official' first day of spring, any more than there are set divisions of the four seasons. The idea of four seasons separated by equinoxes and solstices originated, I understand, from Geminis, a Greek astronomer circa 70 BC. But no one paid much attention to him until, in the last century, the Americans took up the notion, and now celebrate 21st March as the first day of spring.

For convenience one can think of spring as being the months of March, April and May – which I have always thought of as being 'spring' salmon fishing. Summer: June, July, August. Autumn: September, October, November. Winter: December, January and February. But it is all purely arbitrary; it has no scientific basis. The 'spring' weather can be bitterly cold in the valley during March and April and even May, when an east wind whines down from the snow-covered flanks of Scawfell, whereas I have been out at sea-fishing in my shirt sleeves on a calm, sunny day in mid-winter. But then, such seasonal weather eversion comes as no surprise to any countryman in these islands.

Years ago, during 'spring', the door of the garden shed was left open accidentally. Days later we found that the swallows had nipped in and started to build on a ledge just inside the door. So, of course, after that it had to stay open permanently all summer through. They 'set up shop' and in no time, it seemed, there was a family of seven.

It was irritating to start with, but what pleasure those little birds have given us. One is so often unthinking in one's acceptance of nature. The skill and beauty of a bird in flight becomes almost commonplace through repetition; but nowadays when I see those swallows swooping into the shed at a speed so fast that my eyes can scarcely follow their flight, then slowing and turning within the space of only two or three feet before alighting on the nest rim with a beakful of insects for the five baby birds, I realise that what I am watching is an aerial masterpiece.

The swallows see summer in, and they see it out. They did so once in a moment of excitement never to be forgotten. I was standing in the garden watching dozens of them gathering at sunset on the eve of departure. A thunderstorm loomed dark and threatening behind the cottage. Gusting across the valley, the wind plucked off a shower of damson leaves and from a cleft in the clouds a ray of late sunshine slanted across the garden, brilliantly lighting the cottage and throwing the distant fells into even darker shadow. Against that towering purple cumulus, feeding on insects rising from the damp ground, the swallows wheeled and dipped, the last light flashing on their little white bellies, so that in the roaring wind they swirled like sparks from a chimney blown across the sky.

Swallows never cease to fill me with delight. Sometimes, during August evenings as they sit twittering on the telephone wire outside the cottage, I picture them century after century on their fabulous journeys back across the vast stretch of Sahara sands, passing Bedouin camel trains heading for the cool water of the same oasis . . .

But swallows are not built to fly through sandstorms. Only one in three that leave will survive to twitter again on the telephone wires outside the cottage.

All the time they're travelling, swallows feed by snatching insects from the air, so the survival value of flying south to the tropics is obvious – northern Europe is no place for insect eaters in winter. But why ever make the northern journey back? It seems strange programming to return to Europe rather than nest in the balmy weather of the Cape winter.

Today we tend to take the magic of migration for granted. The techniques of modern science have solved much of the mystery of migration routes and distances. But not so long ago the swallows' comings and goings really were considered magical. Their habit of skimming a pool to take a drink on the wing inspired the theory that they dipped underwater and 'conglobulated' in sublacustrine caves. People claimed to have seen them excavated in bushel loads from the mud when ponds were drained.

Where did the swallows go in autumn? Why, they flew to the moon. 'After all,' as one seventeenth century chronicler exclaimed, 'are not the heavens the proper place for birds in winter?'

But the truth is no less impressive than the fiction. A few swallows will make the round journey of twelve thousand miles again and again. One ringed bird is known to have returned for sixteen consecutive years – equivalent in mileage to that mythical journey to the moon.

The truth is perhaps even more spectacular in the case of the young cuckoo that has grown fat in a dunnock's nest in the garden hedge. It is on the point of flying off to East Africa. Just think about that. How will it find its way? Its parents have already gone. This youngster, whose whole life has been spent in the cottage garden, has no one to help it; no one to lead the way and show it where to go. Somehow, it must fly to an exact location in East Africa unaided and alone. And (aided by its genes) fly there it will.

* * *

Equally intriguing is the extraordinary story of what is perhaps the most remarkable of all our migrants, *Anguilla anguilla*. The European eel.

My association with *Anguilla* started long ago. In a boyhood world, when the village stream was a river and the mill-pond an enchanted sea, and summer all sunshine and soft rain and full of song, I fished avidly for eels.

Yes, I knew of other fish. There were roach and perch and carp in the old foundry pool; grey mullet and flounders and sometimes bass swam up the creek among the sea asters where *Neptune*, the converted barge I was brought up on, was moored. But for at least one golden summer in those sun-drenched days of childhood it was the thought of great eels that set my mind on fire. It was the eel, sinister and quiet and sinewy in strength, I went out to catch. And mostly eels I caught.

You may think it strange I should have wished to hook a fish so many people catch and curse when fishing for something else. If so, you still have much to learn. He is a fascinating animal, the eel. And to eat . . . ! However cooked, an epicurean delight. Smoked, not even the salmon can surpass him. But of more importance in those early days was the rough-and-tumble of his capture. He taught me how to fish.

I owe him much. He lured me to exciting places; places of lonely beauty and romance. Tireless in pursuit, I fished those brackish marshland fleets that flashed like knife-blades between the banks of yellow reeds. I followed him to sedge-lined meres, and ancient mill-ponds black and still, with lichen-covered stones and sluice gates thick with weed. I hooked him under canopies of beech and oak, deep in dark owl-haunted woods. Far out on the sun-baked mud flats, I caught him from old Puggy Dimmond's duck-punt as the long, thin stems of bottle-green eel-grass lifted with the tide.

But the world grows. The one horizon I had seen so clearly, faded. Other fish took possession of me. I graduated from the primitive essentials of a bamboo eel-pole to the beauties of a fly rod and the undreamed mysteries of the salmon and the sea trout, and no longer fished the marshland drains for eels. But the magic of that early feeling haunts me still; and perhaps when I am very old I may fish for eels again, and end as I began, among the reeds in contemplation of a float.

*   *   *

There are foolish fishermen who denigrate the eel. Indeed, is any fish so badly treated? I doubt it. For many an angler reeling in that slimy, twisting knot, one look is enough. With the scissors he snips the cast, and bends to his tackle bag to repair the damage – leaving the eel to writhe among the rushes, wrapped in nylon with a hook in its gullet. Many are the eels I have found – and good eels, too – tangled, hooked, and left to die.

No creature should be so barbarously treated. The eel commands respect. In Greek and Latin literature it was the first fish to attain the dignity of a name. And let him who hooks one remember he has hooked a fish whose history is second to none.

To the ancient Greeks, the eel was 'the King of Fish', 'the White Skinned Nymph', 'Goddesses, all clothed in beet' – with which, according to Aristophanes, they were often served. And, highest of all honours: 'the Helen of the Feast!'

Agartharchides, of Knidos, noted that the largest eels from Lake Copais were sacrificed by the Boeothians, who crowned them like human victims and, after sprinkling them with meal, offered prayers over them.

I remember reading somewhere that two crack regiments of the Boeothian army, circa 400 BC were formed entirely of homosexual lovers. Whether a predilection for *Anguilla* played any part in this perverted martial affinity is a matter of conjecture, but from all accounts there can be little doubt that for many people the eel held very special properties.

Freshly-caught, eels were considered an excellent tonic for the voice. And the smoke of burnt eel was said to ease the pangs of childbirth. (Eels are not alone amongst fishes supposed to be supportive in the birth process. According to the *Daily Telegraph* of 4th August, 1992, 'At least twelve women are happy to give birth alongside dolphins in the Red Sea in the belief that the soothing effect of these creatures' presence will make delivery painless.')

To the Egyptians, the eel was sacred – about which Antiphanes wrote:

They say that the Egyptians are clever in that they rank the eel equal to a god, but in reality it is held in esteem and value far higher than gods, for them we can propitiate with a prayer or two, while to get even a smell of an eel at Athens we have to spend 12 drachmae or more!

As food it was the greatest delicacy. One, Philetaerus lamented: When you are dead, you cannot then eat eels.

Enormous prices were paid for eels. The voluptuous Sybarites were so addicted that all persons catching eels were exempt from taxes and tributes.

That charming writer, Arthur Ransome, knew their gastronomic value. Of a day when after big carp, he writes:

Four times the baits were taken by eels, landed amid anathemas, tempered by the thought of next day's breakfast.

Catch *him* cutting them adrift!

As to how eels bred, pretty well every zoologist and fishing writer from Aristotle onwards produced a theory.

Aristotle himself thought they came from inside the earth, forming spontaneously in mud. Oppian wrote:

Strange the formation of the eely race. That knows no sex, yet loves the close embrace.

and thought little eels came from the eel's slime. In Pliny's opinion:

They have no other mode of procreation . . . than by rubbing themselves against rocks – and their scrapings come to life.

Other thinkers attributed the birth of eels to the dew of May mornings, and hair of horses, and gills of fishes. Even the great Izaak Walton plumped for 'Spontaneous Generation – ' but then, not the best of naturalists, he thought that pike bred from pickerel weed.

In *The Fisherman: or The Art of Angling Made Easy* (an appropriation of James Saunders' *The Compleat Fisherman*) Guiniard Charfy observed:

> *There is a greater variety in the Eel than in any other fish of the river, and it is not yet determined how to treat them, whether as a Fish, or as a Reptile. Some, who have no good will to them, put them as no better than a species of Serpents and will call the Water Snakes.*
>
> *Others dispute their Generation, and tell us they are produced not by any spawn, or ova, but by the slime of the earth, impregnated by the heat of the sun; so that they will have them to be only an invigorated corruption and putrefaction. These, and many other nasty notions, these squeamish people have about eels, in order to help their stomachs to loathe them, or at least to justify a pretended aversion to them . . .*
>
> *The Eel has this property, that though they breed in rivers, yet, as they grow bigger, those of them that remove and go down the stream, never attempt to go back again; and those that reach into the sea never return, but continue there till they die, or till they grow to an extraordinary size, and are then called Congers!*

Richardson, writing in 1793, was of the opinion that descending eels went down to the sea to breed. Of the Cumberland Derwent, he remarks:

> *The young eels come up the river in April, in size about the thickness of a common knitting needle.*

That adult eels went into the sea, and young eels came out of it had been noted in Italy in the seventeenth century. But even as late as 1862, we find a Mr D. Cairncross blithely stating:

The progenitor of the Silver eel is a small beetle: of this I feel fully satisfied in my own mind, from a rigid and extensive comparison of its structure and habits with those of other insects.

The first recorded capture of an immature eel was made by a German scientist in the Straits of Messina, in 1856. Not realising what it was, he named it: *Leptocephalus brevirostris* – or, short-snouted thinhead.

In 1896, two Italian scientists discovered that this *Leptocephalus brevirostris* was in fact the larvae of the eel.

The eel's spawning ground in the Sargasso Sea was found by a young Danish marine biologist, Johannes Schmidt, who published his findings in 1921. By means of repeated netting at various depths across the North Atlantic, he drew up a chart showing that the *Leptocephali* he caught became progressively smaller as he approached the Sargasso Sea, where he found the smallest larvae of all.

The story of the European eel's life-cycle is touched with wonder. From that faraway Atlantic birthplace, the tiny eels set off with the Gulf Stream on their three-year eastward drift, during the latter stages of which occurs the metamorphosis from *Leptocephalus* to elver. Then comes the eager thrust into river and stream, as they hurry on towards their genetically computered fresh water destinations.

The male eel stays in fresh water for an average of seven to nine years; the female for ten to twelve years. In one exceptional case a stay of between eighteen and nineteen years has been noted.

After their long years in fresh water, the eels return to sea. In preparation for this journey, the snout (of both sexes) becomes more pointed, the eyes enlarge and develop golden retinal pigments, the back becomes black, and the belly changes from yellow to silver. Almost without exception, the mature female silver eel, which averages about 1lb, is larger than the male – which averages 3 to 4oz, and very rarely exceeds eighteen inches in length.

This migrational change takes about six months to complete. Then, on some dark, stormy autumn night, the eels begin to nose their way down-river towards the sea – and that distant spawning ground nearly four thousand miles away.

Migrating eels seldom move if there is a glimmer of light. They tend to travel only on dark nights, and usually when the river is rising. Referring to silver eels descending from Ullswater, Richardson noted:

Immense quantities are taken in August, September and October in nets at Eel-stank, about half a mile down the river Eamont. In five or six hours, eight or ten horse loads have been caught; but such large quantities only on the darkest and stormiest nights. The largest commonly go last; some have weighed upwards of 9lb. It is worthy of remark that they scarcely stir if the moon peeps out, or when there is lightning; the fishermen even think the light of a candle prevents their motion.

Not so far-fetched as it may seem, that candle-light. Hanging a piece of glowing turf over the gap while they cleared their nets in the darkness was an old Irish eel-fisherman's dodge to prevent eels running past before the nets had been re-set.

Whether eels ever wriggle overland during any part of their seaward journey has been the subject of much controversy. Reliable eye-witness accounts are hard to find. Of great interest therefore, is the experience of a friend, who witnessed an extraordinary mass migration of silver eels to the River Petteril, near Greystoke, in Cumbria; a movement made all the more remarkable by the fact that it happened in bright moonlight. He has given me an account of his experience which, with his kind permission, I quote in full:

It was a warm, damp, autumn evening with a low mist over the river. The sky was clear, with a full moon and very few clouds. The river was at normal height. Between 11pm and midnight, while going from one part of the river to another, I saw a moving shimmering mass in the moonlight. On walking towards this mass I saw that it was a stream of silver eels none of which was more than about a foot long. They kept moving steadily forward through the long wet meadow grass and were not halted by my walking among them, in fact several of them passed over my waders. I followed them to the river and saw them dropping into the water from a steep bank about four feet high. The movement lasted for perhaps five minutes and must have involved several hundred eels.

One very interesting point in this account is the size of the eels, which seems to indicate a mass migration of males. That eels should move at all on a bright clear night is astonishing.

But there it is: an extremely valuable eye-witness account, which affirms that migrating silver eels not only travel overland but will do so in large numbers – sometimes even in moonlight!

There is no biological reason why the eel shouldn't move overland. Experiments have shown that in damp conditions, with the temperature in the region of 15ºC an eel can stay alive out of water for a considerable time, by breathing through its skin.

Altogether, I think you will allow, a remarkable animal – and worthy of our respect.

Finally: savour the words of that seventeenth century literary cleric, Thomas Fuller. On the subject of the Isle of Ely, he observed:

It is said that when the priests of this part of the country would still retain their wives in spite of what Pope and Monks could do to the contrary, their wives and children were miraculously turned into eels, whence it had the name of Ely. I consider it a lie.

Never mind what he considered. Next time you catch an eel, don't cut off the tangled knot and let it wriggle away to death by torture. Reflect that what you have hooked is a creature for whom the Greeks beggared themselves and the Sybarites escaped their taxes; a tonic for the voice, a panacea, a Boeothian sacrifice; an Egyptian god – perhaps, even, the descendant of some sexually incontinent priest!

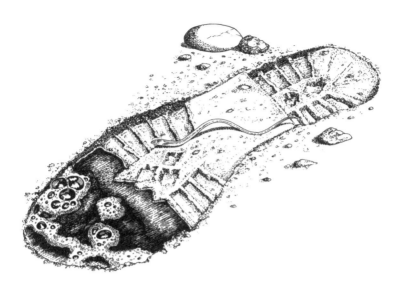

V

ELVER IN DISTRESS

Once in early May, after the swallows (and the cuckoos) had arrived in the valley, I stood beside the river watching thousands upon thousands of baby eels wriggling upstream from the sea.

Somewhere between the Roman fort at Ravenglass and the fort at Hardknott ten miles up the valley, as the fort sites are on opposite banks, the legions must have crossed the river. This crossing place has long been disputed by historians, and nobody is quite sure of the exact location, but wherever it was, there is no doubt that those warriors of old must have witnessed a sight similar to the one I was watching.

Judging by their determination and sense of direction, averaging nine miles a day (though up to thirty miles a day has been recorded) elvers seem to know exactly where they are going. But how? And why? And where?

In the whole of our countryside, few pieces of water are without eels. How is this possible? What directs one particular party of elvers to one particular river or pond? What strange impulse drives one little eel to struggle on and on, mile after mile towards some distant moorland tarn high among the hills, whereas another wriggles into a local ditch? Why don't they all simply go to the same place? Aided by their microscopic brains, but phenomenal sense of smell, do baby eels instinctively find their way to parental waters, like salmon? And the answer is: 'Yes. They do.'

All stories of animal movements are astonishing. This one borders on witchcraft. But as in the case of the swallow and the cuckoo and indeed every other species of animal, it is witchcraft that we call genetic programming (or DNA). And it is no less wonderful for all that. Indeed, the answers science offers to our questions about animal movements create an even greater sense of wonder because ultimately what comes into the arena is the question of life itself.

As St Luke put it: 'Are not five sparrows sold for two farthings, and not one of them is forgotten before God?'

Philosophically (and paradoxically) when we consider the deeper implications of modern scientific research into this genetic programming of migrant animals, the biblical fundamentalist's concept of 'providence in the fall of a sparrow' can no longer be contemptuously dismissed as religious fantasy.

*   *   *

Later, while watching the elver migration up-river, bathed in the valley sunlight of that distant afternoon, I noticed that one little creature had become imprisoned close to the water's edge inside a footprint in the sand. Now, under the hot sun, moisture in the footprint had drained away and the tiny eel's despairing struggles to regain the river had almost ceased. Quickly I scooped it up in my hand, a mere flicker of life remaining, and released it gently in the water. On its return it sank and lay for a time inert on the bottom . . . Until, slowly wavering, it started off again upstream with the elver's typical slow-motion wriggle. I watched it on its way, gaining in strength and speed until eventually it glided between some stones and disappeared.

On my return to the cottage the dogs were in the kitchen, leaping about and barking excitedly. On the window frame, like a dark leaf pressed against the glass, a swallow that had swooped in through the open doorway, crouched terrified. I cursed the dogs and rescued the little creature, happy to find it apparently unharmed.

For a moment, before releasing it outside the door, I gazed in wonder at the tiny, trembling bundle of flesh and skin and feathers that had just flown to the cottage from the bottom of Africa. Then I tossed it high into the air and it soared away in a joyous climbing turn above the chimneypots.

With a strange feeling of elation I watched it go, conscious that for the second time that day I had held a miracle in my hand.

VI
PORTRAIT OF A GENTLEMAN

The celebration of the thirtieth anniversary of the first edition of my book on sea trout fishing was a particular pleasure, because my connection with the publishing house of H.F. & G. Witherby went back more than thirty years and that, in angling terms, is a long time.

In those days, shoals of salmon and sea trout lay thick in the cottage pools and I am often accused of exaggeration when looking back with nostalgia to such exciting times.

But in my little world it really was like that. Not only the beautiful little valley river where I lived but all the other local rivers teemed with fish, and enchanted bog-myrtle-scented summer sea trout nights succeeded each other in a sequence of almost uninterrupted magic. To make a living as and how I pleased in such a lovely place with private fishing at my door, was paradise.

Paradise indeed. But it was a paradise hard won. Making a living independently 'as and how I pleased', with no money in the bank and accepting no help whatever from any form of social security, was neither as easy nor idyllic as it sounds.

Although the hardship of my years of wartime captivity had prepared me both mentally and physically for life without electricity in a remote country cottage, with a primitive system of sanitation based on a highly idiosyncratic water supply piped from a fellside beck, there were times when I began to wonder whether I would ever succeed in picking up the professional threads of my life which were severed when I married Kathleen and left London for good.

These were the years before I re-started a career in radio and television, mainly by writing and producing wildlife programmes, and was scraping a living from intermittent hack-work, which in the circumstances proved difficult and precarious.

Always short of money and sometimes penniless, we never-theless struggled along as best we could. For a time in the late 1950s, as described in my book *Sea Trout Fishing*, we took in paying guests, mostly fellwalkers and anglers, turning my study into a temporary bedroom and letting out our upstairs rooms. And there were also times when I found myself having to work as a labourer in a factory or on a building site for the money to help tide us over difficult patches in winter.

But we were strong and fit and happy in our way of life, which was as near to completely natural freedom and independence as I think it possible to find in this overcrowded island.

None of this would have been workable without the unquenchable faith and support of my wife, Kathleen. And you will understand, I hope, and sympathise with the feeling of pride engendered by our attempt to live as much as possible off the land – depending on my rods and my gun and on that weird alchemy called 'green fingers' which enabled Kathleen to produce such a profusion of fruit and vegetables (as well as flowers) from what I have described in an earlier chapter as our 'garden'.

And there were two other points that made this way of life possible: we owned the cottage we lived in with no mortgage, and we had a stretch of fishing on the river.

Fortunate in having free fishing, I set about enjoying it to the best of my ability. Between intensive bouts of work, I fished with limitless enthusiasm day after day, night after night, whenever I was able, the seasons through. The runs of fish seemed inexhaustible and my sporting diary – which recorded catches inconceivable today – provided the backbone for *Sea Trout Fishing*, my first volume on angling – which was written entirely during the still watches of the night in winter.

In due course it was to H.F. & G. Witherby that the manuscript was sent with a view to publication.

I knew Witherby's reputation as publishers of ornithological and sporting books, and can re-live the excitement of receiving a letter from the firm's managing director, Antony Witherby, informing me of his interest in my work.

This was splendid stuff. All the same, flattering though it was to have gained the attention of such reputable publishers, I was worried about the book's future. Based on years of angling research and observation, what I had written would, I felt sure, take time to be appreciated and I sensed the urgency of ensuring its survival. Realising, however, that this would be impossible to arrange by letter or on the telephone, I decided that a meeting in London was essential.

And so it happened that, albeit reluctantly, I left my enchanted valley and travelling south, came at last to the somewhat tenebrous City building which, in those days, housed the prestigious publishing firm of Witherby.

Stumbling on frayed oilcloth, I threaded my way through a passage piled with dusty books – remaindered dreams, presumably, of earlier authors. Disturbed by my approach a spider scuttled across the floor narrowly missing my foot, an incident that comes readily to mind because spiders terrify me and this one (undoubtedly a *Teginaria* female) was huge.

Journey's end, reminiscent of a literary hat-box, was a small but lofty office, lined with books. From behind a massive desk tucked away in a corner beneath a fanlight already grey with dust, Witherby's managing director peered out at me with bright, unwinking eyes. A cup of tea materialised and after courteous greetings I was offered a cigarette, a rather uncomfortable chair and a biscuit.

Apart from a morbid dread of spiders and fear of lightning, I am not by nature a nervous disposition, but by now my confidence – which had got roughed-up during that journey through the remaindered books – was getting ragged. Somehow my biscuit had found its way into the teacup. There was no spoon, and I sat fiddling nervously as the Great Publisher lit a cigarette and eyed me for a while in silence.

I am well aware how time distorts the memory of events long past, but this first meeting with Antony Witherby was one of the most momentous happenings of my life. So you will understand that, as though set in glass, the essence of what passed between us has remained forever vivid.

"Mr Falkus," the great man said at length, tapping a folder on the desk. "I have read your manuscript. It is very interesting. Very. With your permission I would like to publish it."

"Thank you," I said. "That's fine. I'm delighted. That really is great news. But . . ." I paused. This was the moment of truth and I needed to summon all my courage. "I have one very important stipulation."

"A stip-u-lation?"

"Yes," I said boldly. "If you are going to publish my book you must promise to keep it in print for at least ten years."

As if turned to stone, Mr Witherby sat stunned. And I can understand pretty well how he felt. Although only dimly conscious of it at the time, I realise now the absurdity of my demand. To agree to keep a book in print for a decade or more purely on an author's speculation is something no present-day publisher would dream of doing. Perhaps, like our rivers, the book trade was different then. I don't know. And at the time I didn't care. I had been rehearsing my speech all the way to London, and now it came tumbling out.

"Please don't think me conceited," I implored, spreading my hands. "But I've been fishing all my life and what I've written in this book on sea trout is unlike anything ever printed. I know most of it is about night fishing. But then, the techniques of catching sea trout by day are relatively straightforward. Fishing for these creatures at night is something completely different. In the whole range of angling there is nothing remotely like it. Sea trout night fly fishing demands its own special tackle and methods and approach. It is a fabulously wonderful sport entirely of its own and nothing to do with brown trout or salmon fishing. And to be perfectly frank, from what I've read, nobody seems to know very much about it." I leaned forward, seized the manuscript and riffled through its pages. "If you publish this book in the usual way, like most sporting books are published, selling a thousand or so copies, clearing a small profit and then allowing it to be remaindered, it will be dead in six months and forgotten inside twelve. You see, so far as I know, most of the methods in this book are entirely new and I believe it will be at least ten years before people begin to understand what I've written. And for that to happen it has to be in print."

Antony Witherby nodded slowly, pressing the points of his fingers together and tilting backwards in his chair. There was a long silence. The traffic in the street sounded faint and faraway, the office seemed shadowy and insubstantial. I watched, fascinated, as Mr Witherby tilted further and further back, staring intently at the ceiling. Although I hardly suspected it then, it is probable that my future reputation as an angling writer hung on the outcome of those few moments.

What concerned me at the time, however, was that if my host leaned back much further there could be a nasty accident, perhaps fatal, and my journey to London would be wasted. A selfish thought, perhaps, but, as I have learned since, all writers if not already self-centred become so the moment they complete a book.

Then, with a thud, Antony Witherby's chair swung forward, and I breathed again.

"Mr Falkus," he said carefully. "I have listened with great attention to what you have to say and I will make a bargain with you. I will undertake to do exactly as you ask, if you, on your part, will promise me something in return."

He paused, eyeing me keenly.

"This manuscript," he went on, tapping the file. "It is an original work and very well written, but it is only a skeleton of the book I feel certain you can write. I will publish it and keep it in print for ten years, as you request, but then I shall expect you to put the flesh on these bones and write me the expanded second edition they deserve. Will you do it?"

Would I not!

* * *

But . . . for a professional writer the income from most sporting books is depressingly meagre, and as an almost penniless film-maker who devoted nearly every spare moment to fishing, I found little time to write about it. Anyway I had no burning ambition to become an angling pundit. What I had already written on the subject of sea trout was surely sufficient.

Nevertheless I had made a bargain, and with the passing years, like the anguish of Doctor Faustus, tortured thoughts of my compact with Antony Witherby began to nag. All this time he had kept *Sea Trout Fishing* advertised and in print. But although I was conscious of my debt, with a steady increase in television and radio work, the discipline of sitting down to the long slog necessary for building a big second edition became more and more onerous.

As season followed season the precepts offered in my first edition began to be practised and understood by a growing number of anglers. Slowly the sales of the book increased until, quite suddenly, it had sold out – and I found myself faced with five hundred pages of a second edition on which I had not yet inscribed one word.

To save the ship, my patient but practical publisher plastered the hole up with a reprint. At which I breathed a sigh of relief – and started work on a lucrative film script.

But my respite was short-lived. The reprint of *Sea Trout Fishing* sold out very quickly and the day soon came when, tired of making telephone excuses on my behalf in answer to Antony Witherby's repeated enquiries, my wife Kathleen finally lost her temper.

"Listen!" She said. "Tony's done everything he promised, and more. You don't know how lucky you are. Nobody else would have kept your book going all these years, but he did. And now he wants the new edition, and you haven't written a single word of it. Well, you must. He's done what he promised to do, and it's time you did the same!"

After that there was nowhere to hide.

* * *

As things turned out, the second edition was an immediate success, going through one impression after another. It was followed, in a glow of self-righteousness, with *Salmon Fishing* – another work I had rashly promised, but failed to produce, some years before.

This, too, proved a winner. (After eight years, I am proud to say, it is in its tenth impression and selling better than ever.) And it is to the man responsible for all this that I am privileged, publicly, to have been given the chance of declaring my thanks.

Down towards the tail of a pool in the river below my home, Cragg Cottage, is a large submerged stone called Witherby's Rock. It gained its name, years ago, because whenever Tony Witherby came to stay and waded that pool for sea trout, he invariably fell over it. So far as I remember, he never did fish the pool tail right out. After the splashdown he would head back to the cottage for a bath.

I was reminded of it while writing this piece and thinking of his own rock-like qualities during our long association, and how steadfastly he had stuck to his agreement. I shall never cease to be grateful for the help he gave me. What a lucky star lit my way along that dark London corridor all those years ago. Without his inspiration it is unlikely that *Sea Trout Fishing* and *Salmon Fishing* in their present forms would ever have been written.

So now I take this opportunity of telling all those readers who so kindly express their pleasure in my books, that the person who deserves most of their thanks is not me. It is someone who, during the disintegration of the degenerate Sixties, behaved like a gentleman and kept his word.

VII
THE ISLAND OF GEESE

Before setting off for the mainland I wandered with Sean through the ruins of the tiny village, listening to his account of this strange primitive settlement which had eked out a precarious existence here on the edge of the world before, eventually, tragedy overtook it.

Caught by the setting sun, the ancient Celtic cross, leaning drunkenly on top of its knoll, threw a long, slanting shadow across the sands. Then, suddenly, as we came out on a sweep of open grassland, I realised we were walking on a carpet of what looked like dried-up goose droppings.

"Do wild geese come here in the winter?" I asked.

"Oh, they do," said Sean. He pointed towards the smudge of distant shore line. "It's the barnacles and the greylags you understand, they come from the land to feed on this grass. There must be something about it they like. They come every year. That's why this is called the 'Island of Geese.'"

*   *   *

The MFV chugged steadily across the long, slow Atlantic swell with the shark's carcass lashed alongside. There was the palest line of dull red on the western horizon, the sky now a clear velvet blue becoming full of stars. A swathe of phosphorescent brilliance, caused by *noctaluca*, the microscopic luminous planktonic creatures, had erupted in a brief firework display of sparkling light, streaming back from the bows and along the seaward side of the shark.

Feeling sorry for myself, I sat apart from the film crew, alone on the cuddy hatch, nursing my aching body, staring out across the darkening sea and trying to revive my leaden spirit with gulps from a bottle of Scotch. I thought of that poor great harmless creature we had made fast alongside, dying in a welter of blood and foam. For what? To provide a vicarious thrill for a peanut-crunching public sitting in a cheap-scented cinema.

To do it, I had risked my life. One mistake could have drowned me. A loop of rope catching round an ankle while the shark was running would have wrenched me overboard and dragged me down. But what about it? It hadn't. Though I felt no sense of pride. It was simply my job; something which, in the circumstances, I had to do. Well the deed was done.

I had got the dramatic scene needed to complete the story. Oh, the film would sell now, there was no doubt about that. It would make money, perhaps quite a lot of money, which would be shared between two shattered women whose children could be looked after, fed and clothed and educated. So, by fighting the shark and killing it I suppose in one sense I had succeeded. But in the state of mind I was in, it was an achievement that left me feeling empty and sick and, in a strange way, ashamed.

After a time, as the level of the bottle sank and numbed the pain, the feeling of self-pity left me, and my spirits rose. Well, I thought, at least I had given Hemingway's Old Man of the Sea something to think about. I looked landwards towards the loom of the distant hills, seeing the clear summer sky scudding with cloud and hearing, with sudden longing, the magic clamour of wild geese flighting to the island under a winter moon. Perhaps they might clear my mind of horrors, if I had the will-power to return. Well, I had done so once, for the sake of others. Surely I could do it for myself? I knew then that one day I would come back.

VIII
ISLAND ADVENTURE

Depend upon it, the thought that you are about to drown concentrates the mind wonderfully. And I have no doubt that this paraphrase of the great doctor's axiom is generally true. Nevertheless, what concentrated my mind so wonderfully when the skiff foundered off the deserted Atlantic island in that long-ago December dusk, was not so much the preservation of my life, as the preservation of my wellies.

The customary advice offered by the literature to anyone falling into deep water wearing wellingtons, is to kick them off at once. But there I was, two hundred yards from shore, struggling to keep mine on. The truth was that, ill-fitting though they happened to be, if I lost those boots I had nothing else to wear. The boxes holding my spare clothes, and indeed most of my comestibles, were lying on the bottom in five fathoms.

Of my subsequent adventures, more later. Sufficient now to remind my reader that while harpooning sharks off the island in the summertime two years before and discovering it to be a winter haunt of wild geese, I had resolved to land there again one day for some shooting. Now, I was in the process of realising that ambition, and so far the landing had been a lemon.

Jimmy and Sean, who brought me from the mainland in the MFV, had helped to beach the first curragh-load of supplies and carry it all up to the hut. After which, we returned to the MFV and loaded the curragh with turf and my other luggage. Then, as the weather looked ominous and the short winter day was drawing-in, they had cast me off and, assuming I was happy, turned and headed for home.

Indeed, at the moment of parting I was happy enough. As they rounded the island out of sight they waved goodbye, and I waved back. A minute or so later, with nothing between me and Labrador, I found myself swimming for my life.

It was the craziest accident. Loading that turf into the curragh had knocked the bung out! From then on, unseen under the growing mound of turf bags, the boat had been steadily filling, so that one moment I was sculling contentedly shorewards; the next, the turf was floating off all round me as the curragh went under.

Needless to say, I looked hopefully towards the headland and shouted. But my voice was blown away on the wind. Despairingly I realised I could expect no help from that quarter; Jimmy and Sean were on their way and had no reason to turn back. There was no longer anyone living on the island.

Any future I had was entirely in my own hands.

When everything had fallen or been washed out of it, the waterlogged curragh re-surfaced and I started to swim it in towards the shore, hanging on to the transom and kicking with my legs. Not easy with wellies on, but I had to do the best I could. And you will understand that since those borrowed boots were the only footwear to survive the accident, I was at some pains to preserve them.

Reaching the shallows, I pulled the boat up through the surf, rocked most of the water out of it, baled out the remainder and rolled the hull part way up the beach on the oars. Lumps of turf were bobbing all along the water's edge. I salvaged as much of it as I could, throwing it up on the strand. Then I carried it all to the hut and heaped it in a pile by the door. Precious stuff, that peat: there was little else immediately available to burn.

Fortunately, the load of stores I had already landed included my gun, cartridges, blankets, matches and five-gallon drum of paraffin. But only one box of eatables had survived, and I listened to the rising wind with a sudden premonition that what food there was would have to last much longer than originally intended.

By now the late dusk had turned to darkness. Inside the hut's only room I lit a candle, poured paraffin on wet sticks and turf blocks and heaped more blocks in the open hearth. At last, to my great relief, a flame leaped up, and the fire started that, from then on, I never let go out.

A rusty iron chain with a hook in the end dangled from the chimney. I filled the kettle at the tiny stream that flowed through the ruined village and hung it over the flames. By now

I was shivering violently, so I stripped off my soaking clothes, rinsed the saltwater out of them in the stream and spread them by the fire to dry. Then I wrapped myself in my blankets and climbed into the rickety wooden bunk.

During the many days of rough weather that followed, I was to spend a lot of time in that bunk – each time I got wet, in fact, as my spare clothes were lost, and so were my oilskins. Every stitch of clothing I had with me was steaming in front of that fire.

To be frank, the planning of this adventure – which left so much to be desired – had got badly worn the night before in Sweeney's bar. As the evening 'developed' I had become more and more scornful of the long list of gear and provisions friends had advised my taking. Had it not been for this arrogance, I would have been considerably better equipped. As it was, I knew now that, if the weather stayed bad, my foolishness, combined with the accident to the curragh was likely to turn what had started as a lighthearted jaunt into one hell of a struggle.

At the time, however, although hubris had deservedly been met by Nemesis, I was far from feeling deflated. By immense good fortune a case of Scotch had escaped the landing disaster. I poured myself a glass and lay tucked up in my blankets feeling absurdly relaxed and happy.

My living quarters were small. The hut, used occasionally by the shark fishermen, consisted of a single room with an open fireplace, a bunk, a table and a window with four square panes of glass. One pane had a hole in it the size of a cricket ball, and to stem the draught I had plugged this hole with a piece of screwed-up newspaper. That done, and a fire blazing, the hut soon became quite snug and warm, and solitude closed round me.

All this happened during the days before I went to live at Cragg Cottage, and after the hurly-burly of London life it was a superb feeling to be alone on a desert island. No insistent telephone or roar of traffic; no one to nag. Only the age-old elemental sounds of wind and sea, and the rain hissing in the chimney. No matter what had happened today, I was safe and sound. Tomorrow could look after itself.

Drowsy in the warmth of the glowing turf, I lay listening to the wind whining in the empty ruins. The island had a long history of occupation and I started thinking about its possible connection with St Columba one thousand five hundred years ago. The worthy saint is reputed to have lived on it for a time before founding his monastry on Iona. A poem attributed to him begins:

> *Delightful would it be to sit on the pinnacle of*
> *a rock,*
> *That I might often see the face of the*
> *ocean . . .*

And goes on to tell of:

> *The Sea Monsters, the greatest of all wonders*

Now what did he mean by that, I pondered, pouring myself another Scotch. Could he have been referring to grey seals? Columba from all accounts was not the sort of chap to indulge in fanciful hyperbole. A grey seal can scarcely be considered a 'monster'. If he wrote about 'monsters', monsters he undoubtedly meant. In all likelihood, monsters he must have seen.

And after all, why not? There are many eye-witness reports of huge sea monsters; humped serpent-like creatures, or giant cuttlefish reputedly responsible for sinking small sailing ships.

Perhaps Columba wrote his poem on this very island. With its Atlantic setting it seemed a likely place for 'monsters' to come ashore. I could imagine something horrendous creeping out of the water and slithering across the sand towards the hut; the ill-fitting door slowly opening; a slimy tentacle insinuating itself across the floor towards me . . .

I shivered. Suddenly the temperature in the room seemed to have dropped.

It had. The ball of newspaper plugging the hole in the window had disappeared, and a current of cold night air was blowing across my neck.

'Hell!' I thought. 'The wind must have blown that paper into the room.'

But it hadn't.

Search as I might, that paper ball was not inside the hut. Puzzled, I tore off another piece, crumpled it up, pushed it into the hole and returned to my bunk.

But, even as I pulled the blankets round me, I felt an icy draught on my face. I looked up. The hole in the window was empty!

Odd! Very odd!

My feeling of well-being vanished. Up to now I had been too occupied to notice the surrounding atmosphere. It was, I suddenly realised with a quickening of the pulse, distinctly eerie.

Again I searched for the missing ball of paper. Again I searched in vain. Again I plugged the hole with a sheet of newspaper. And again, with a strange feeling of disquiet, climbed back in my bunk.

Then, as I twitched the blankets once more around my naked shoulders, something made me glance up at the window . . . and for a moment my heart stopped.

Silhouetted against the grey windowpanes, a great flat head, followed by a long neck reared slowly up. As I watched, transfixed, it seized the ball of newspaper and sank down again. Through the hole in the window a draught of cold night air wisped into the room.

To say I was frightened would be a laughable understatement. Petrified, I sat rigid, clutching the sides of the bunk. But although my body was momentarily frozen, my mind was racing. However prolonged the previous night in Sweeney's, what I had just seen was no figment of a hung-over and fevered imagination. Something had snitched that ball of newspaper, and whatever had done it was lurking just outside the hut. To find out what, I had only to open the door and confront it.

'*Only*'! It was, I reckon an act of considerable courage.

Without being conscious of moving, I found myself beside the door. Opening it a fraction, I peered out. There was nothing to be seen.

For a moment I began to doubt my sanity. Then I heard a sort of snuffling sound, and realised with an icy feeling up the back of my neck that something was moving just out of sight round the corner of the hut.

Cautiously, oh so cautiously, I crept outside the door, edged my way to the corner . . . and peeped round. No more than a couple of yards from me, ears flattened back, was the monster itself. A small donkey.

I stood staring at it. Ears laid back chewing gently as it swallowed the last of the *Irish Times*, the donkey stood and stared at me. Then it turned abruptly and trotted off into the darkness.

What was this unlikely animal doing on the island? Whence had it come? Whither had it gone? I didn't know the answer to any of these questions, then. And frankly, I didn't care. Feeling rather foolish but conscious of intense relief, I returned to my bunk and poured myself another large Scotch.

*　*　*

Place yourself alone on a deserted island and time assumes a new dimension. Certainly on the treeless, humped splinter of Atlantic rock and sand and grass that held me weather-bound throughout those long-ago December days, the change was quite uncanny. Even during the short hours of winter daylight I never seemed rushed to get anything done. Should I decide to carve a spoon, build a dry-stone goose hide, stalk a rabbit or construct a dam, time expanded or contracted to fit the job in hand.

Hunger was the only conflict. I could dine as and when I wished – provided there was something to eat. As my meagre store of provisions dwindled, what started out as a lighthearted sporting adventure became a matter of survival.

In essence, of course, the whole of one's life is simply a matter of filling in time between meals. However we may choose to earn a living or to enjoy ourselves, we have to eat. We can please ourselves how we live and for whatever lofty motives. But if we don't eat, we die. And although for many of us, in the Western world the edges are softened by the trappings of modern civilisation, when hunger obtrudes, most of these trappings disappear.

Most, but not all. There was, for instance, my hot shower.

An improbable luxury in such primitive surroundings? Not really; it was very simple to construct. The tide-line provided two empty drums, one conveniently smaller than the other. I opened them up, scrubbed them clean with sand, knocked holes in the bottom of the smaller drum, tied on a wire rope (from some of the shark fishermen's gear stored in the hut) and placed it inside the larger drum which, for each bath, was filled with water from the stream and heated by a driftwood fire on a stone grate inside one of the ruins. At the appropriate temperature I stripped off, hauled up the smaller drum on a derrick fashioned from a fallen beam, swung it to one side and stood underneath, letting the hot water dribble down my back. A great contentment, and very soothing on a raw day.

Fuel was the only problem. Driftwood proved surprisingly scarce. Only one little bay held any to speak of, and Sod's Law positioned that on the furthermost tip of the island.

That wouldn't have mattered since there was nothing to do once my next meal was assured except go beachcombing. But my only footwear to survive the landing disaster when the skiff foundered was that ill-fitting pair of borrowed wellingtons, and walking became increasingly painful.

In desperation I cut off the toes. This brought instant relief, but toeless wellies let the water in, and December is no month to walk about wet-footed.

Then occurred one of those bizarre incidents that challenge belief in an ordered universe and invoke visions of the supernatural. While searching for driftwood, I found, half-buried on the tide-line, an enormous boot. A giant's boot. Size 14 at least. Fifty yards further on, unbelievingly, I found its mate.

Seized with wonder, I prised them from the sand, washed them out and, like Crusoe faced with Man Friday's footprint, stood and meditated on their origin.

I stand six feet and wear size 10s. But these were a good four or five sizes bigger. Who could possibly have feet large enough to fit them? And what of his mental condition? They seemed almost new. Surely, only an idiot would throw such boots away? Like the 'monster' that had so dramatically greeted me on my arrival, was he still lurking somewhere on the island? A deranged giant seemed no less likely than a newsprint-eating donkey. It was a chilling thought.

Never mind. I had needed boots, and boots Fate had provided. So, perhaps Fate would continue to 'protect me without my stir'. I carried my treasures back to the hut, stuffed them with cardboard and tied them on with string. Henceforth I wore them constantly, shuffling about the island and deriving absurd pleasure from the line of preposterous footprints they left behind me in the sand.

As day followed day, time passed pleasantly enough. I was alone but seldom lonely. Although the supply of newspaper was exhausted, the donkey had become quite a chum and turned up most days to look hopefully at the broken window. Then there were the choughs.

I had never before seen choughs in the flesh. Jolly, crow-like little birds. In size, half-way between rook and jackdaw, with curved, thin beaks, red-orange in colour like the legs. There were four of them, very tame and very noisy. Chattering incessantly, they spent most of their time sitting on the hut, or just outside the door on a baulk of timber I used as a chopping-block.

Early in our relationship I gave them a slice of my precious bread, cutting it into little cubes and putting it on the block outside the door. It disappeared in a flash, while my back was turned.

I was staggered. 'Poor little birds,' I thought. 'They must be starving.' I cut off another slice, chopped it up and put it outside.

Again, a moment later when I looked round the bread had vanished.

This was incredible. Such avian voracity would be fascinating to observe, so I cut off yet a third precious slice. This time, keeping back out of sight, I stayed and watched.

Almost immediately, round the end of the hut a familiar head appeared and, while the choughs protested excitedly, a long pale tongue swept up the bread.

"Oh, Moke," I said sadly, as he stood there, chewing. "You bugger!" Then I shrugged. Why grudge him food? One day, if the gales persisted, I might have to eat that donkey.

So far, however, things hadn't got as desperate as that. There were still plenty of geese flighting to the island, and rather surprisingly there were a few rabbits – presumably introduced by someone sometime in the distant past. Mind you, you can tire of boiled goose pretty quickly. Rabbits, too, begin to pall after you've eaten half-a-dozen. My diet was leavened to a small extent by the occasional mallard, and I could have had snipe. But when you are hunting for the pot with limited cartridges, snipe shooting is unprofitable.

I had no idea how long I might stay marooned. It was quite possible for this unexpected bad weather to persist all winter. So, when the chances came during daylight, to conserve ammunition goose-stalking replaced flighting. In time I got quite good at it. Crawling about after geese can be most exciting, and one's fierce elation at bringing off a successful shot is heightened by the thought that dinner depended on it.

By the very nature of its geography, a deserted island condemns one to isolation. But this has its compensations. The sense of helpless frustration that so often darkens one's daily life disappears. Within that constricting ring of sea exists a new and unaccustomed freedom. There are no phantoms to haunt 'with tart disparagings', or 'chiding loud at the fall of the night', and there is liberty enough.

In contrast to the frenetic daily round and largely artificial values of London life, my island existence gave me the solitude and freedom Fate provided later in the Cumbrian valley I was destined to inhabit for so many years – a sense of living within touch of reality. Besides, I had plenty of Scotch.

'Call no man happy until he is dead,' said Solon the wise, the Great Athenian legislator, seventh century BC, 'He is at best but fortunate.'

Fortunate to have landed safely on the island I may have been. But sitting in my goose-hide pondering Solon's legendary wisdom, I couldn't help feeling that notwithstanding his belief in a better life to come, he was being unduly atrabilious when he let that one go.

My concept of immediate happiness has always hung on the reply to a simple question: whether in any given situation, at that particular time, there is any other place I would prefer to be; anything else I would rather be doing. If the answer is 'no' then, whatever the context, I reckon to be as happy as can reasonably be expected.

Asking myself that question as I sat contentedly with my gun in the wan December sunshine watching a party of greylags circling the hide, I realised with a selfish but comforting glow of satisfaction that, although spartan in its comfort, my present hermit-like existence was very happy indeed.

*   *   *

At sunset on Christmas Eve it was still blowing hard from the south-west and the distant hill tops were black with cloud. Then the mainland was blotted out as rain came scudding across the sea. There was no half-light of dusk. One moment the mountains were a smudge above the dunes, then it was dark.

As I clumped along the strand in those enormous boots, heading into the rain, spindrift from the reef swept across my face like smoke. By the time I reached the hut I was drenched. After heaping turf blocks high in the open hearth with a liberal dose of paraffin, I hung the kettle on its chain above the flames and stripped off my sodden clothes. Then, when they were squeezed out and hung to dry, I brewed a jug of tea and lay wrapped in blankets by the fireside, watching raindrops fall from the chimney and hiss on the glowing turf.

Later, after moonrise, geese would flight in to feed on the short, sweet grass behind the ruined village. But until then there was time to rest, and reflect.

For many centuries, according to the account of an octogenarian Mayo man who had once lived there, the island had maintained a tiny population bound by its own dialect and laws and, indeed, its own 'king'. Once, there had been a small monastic settlement – whose carved stone slab with its Celtic cross still leaned from a knoll behind the hut. The monks departed a thousand years ago, but at some time during the following centuries the island was re-occupied. The years passed quietly enough, but somewhere along the line the inhabitants, it seems, acquired a rather strange custom. Staunch Catholics though they were, fishing was their way of life; and like all fishermen, exposed by the nature of their trade to constant danger, they were highly superstitious.

This is not surprising. They braved the Atlantic in home-built curraghs, and superstition is understandable in men separated from eternity by thin wooden frameworks covered with tarred canvas.

Certainly for them the Church was not enough. Life hereafter was one thing. Life on earth quite another. For their protection here and now – or, to be more precise, for the safety of the curragh crews while herring fishing – they relied on something more tangible.

According to the Mayo man, this was nothing other than a ship's figure-head on a pole, swathed in red flannel. But to those remote island fisherfolk living on the edge of nowhere, it was Aeolus himself: a symbol of compassion that calmed the sea and bade the wind sing softly.

They called this deity the 'New Woge' – which, although meaning and spelling are obscure, is as near as I can get to the pronunciation.

The protective powers of the New Woge were ineffectual, it seemed, unless everyone available combined in suitable supplication. This entailed setting the thing up on the strand, lighting a bonfire and dancing round it singing 'a joyous song'.

Well, one day when the weather turned dicey with the curraghs still at sea, this act of idolatry was witnessed by a visiting Victorian journalist – who wrote a scandalised account. This came to the notice of the local bishop, who despatched a priest full speed to ensure the islanders' immediate return to the fold.

The priest duly arrived in a six-oared curragh, subjected his wayward flock to several days of moral castigation and ordered the 'heathen idol' to be burnt forthwith.

To his dismay this demand met with flat refusal. They were, they said, devout Christians. The New Woge was just something a bit extra: it had done them very well up to now thank you, and they had no intention of destroying it.

After hours of argument the priest was forced to compromise. They could, he conceded, retain the New Woge, provided they took it down from the wall of the tiny church where they kept it, and buried it in the graveyard. This was done, and thankfully he summoned his oarsmen and headed for the mainland.

And it happened that as his curragh left the island a sudden storm blew up. Exposed to the full force of the Atlantic, and baling furiously, the Reverend Father found himself being swept nearer and nearer to the rocks. Just when all seemed lost, the villagers – who had been watching thoughtfully – rushed to the graveyard, dug up the New Woge and dragged it to the strand. While some gathered fuel for a fire, others capered round the pole singing the 'joyous song' that only they could sing. And by curious chance the wind dropped and the man of God came safely ashore – to be greeted by jubilant islanders insisting that their claim could no longer be refuted and what did he think of the New Woge now?

Knowing he was beaten, and being a realist, he made a deal with them: that they could do what they liked with their New Woge, provided it was never again witnessed by anyone outside the island.

*   *   *

Above the strand where once the New Woge stood, I dozed beside the fire in my hut. At midnight, an hour after moonrise, wearing one of my blankets like a toga – sweater and reefer-jacket still being wet – I heaped some of the few remaining blocks of turf on the embers and went out into the night.

The clouds were drifting northwards more slowly now, and the rain had stopped. In the south-east was a circle of pale moonlight. The gale was easing, and in consideration of my dwindling fuel supply, I sensed thankfully that my time on the island was coming to an end.

Thinking about the past, I wandered through the ruined vil-lage. Hundreds of years of history lay among the tumbled stones of those tiny dwellings. For centuries the people who lived there had wrenched an existence from the island's thin soil and from the sea. They had lived, as it were, in a time capsule, enduring almost unbelievable hardship with only the barest of necessities. Now, unless they had ghosts that walked, they were gone for ever, and in the roofless, sand-filled dwellings where once they lived and made love and died, only the moonlight lingered. What had been their lives, their thoughts, their ambitions, their beliefs? Had they really danced to an idol that calmed the sea and brought the curraghs safely home?

Well, if so, it failed them once. Or did it?

The tragedy happened early in this century, when a freak storm blew up from flat calm one lazy autumn evening. With a four-man crew, every available curragh was out herring fishing to the south of the island. I heard the story first-hand from the Mayo man, the last survivor of that terrible night. We met briefly, just the once, shortly before he died. I understood what he said only through an interpreter.

The storm, he told me, had risen with frightening swiftness from the east – the most dangerous of all quarters, for it blows straight offshore. Taken by surprise, most of the curragh crews struggled desperately to save their nets, their most precious possessions, and started to haul them in. None of them succeeded. Too late, they cut the nets adrift. But so violent was the storm that those boats not already swamped by the breaking seas, were swept westwards like skimming-dishes into the vastness of the Atlantic.

Only the Mayo man's boat survived. At the first sign of the weather change, with astonishing prescience, and considerable moral courage considering the value of what he was abandoning, the skipper cut their net loose and bade his crew head straight for the island. They lived. Every other island fisherman at sea was drowned.

Their curraghs, built on traditional lines, were buoyant and seaworthy craft – within their limits – but extremely light and with scanty draft. To avoid being slapped broadside-on to a sea and swamped, they had to be kept head-to-wind. Boats as light as that cannot 'carry their way'. Row as hard as they could, the men were swept three yards to leeward for every yard they gained to windward, a distance that would increase as the gale worsened and the men grew weaker.

Three bodies from one indomitable crew were found washed-up on a rocky headland of an island twenty miles down the coast: their finger bones white where the flesh was worn from their hands, so hard had they tried to row to safety against the storm.

*   *   *

Let there be no misunderstanding, I believe neither in ghosts nor any form of after-life, but I must confess that while standing alone with my thoughts in that primitive and eerie place among the sand-filled, moonlit ruins of what had once been a busy huddle of human habitation, I felt an atmosphere crowding my senses, a heightening of my imagination. I was like the chap who said that although he didn't for one moment believe in ghosts, it didn't stop him being very frightened of them. It was not only the scantiness of my clothing and the cutting wind that made me shiver. The surviving islanders, old folk, women and children had, I knew, been taken off the island by the government a year or two later and re-housed in a settlement on the mainland. But why had it all happened? Where had been the New Woge in their menfolk's greatest hour of need? Had its potency been diminished by the Holy Father? Had his strictures taken root? Had the islanders really become 'enlightened' and burnt their Great Protector after all?

So many questions left unanswered. Only the Mayo man could have told me. And now, alas, he too had gone. As with so many opportunities in my life, I had missed the chance that would never come again.

Then, suddenly, a sound of singing mingled with the crash of breakers on the beach and my heart gave a sickening jump as, in the same instant, the strand flickered with light and I smelt the unmistakable scent of fresh turf smoke . . .

Fool! The smoke was from my own fire, the flames were moonlight, the chanting only wind whining in the ruined walls.

But then, faintly, as I listened, above the sound of wind and sea I heard a murmur in the sky: a conversation impossible to confuse. Far out across the water the geese were flighting. Once or twice I distinguished the deeper notes of greylags, but mostly they were barnacles – talking as they flew with their sharp yelping call, which is like the baying of young hounds.

The sound swelled to a crescendo. A patchwork shadow swept across the shore, white feathers shining briefly in the moonlight as the skeins swung round overhead with the rustle of wind in autumn leaves. Circling, the geese gradually lost height, until at last they settled on the bare grassland with a sigh of wings. And the night was full of their clamour.

Seawards, in a swathe of moonlight across the waters where I had killed the shark, and where once a cluster of desperate curragh crews with bleeding hands had fought the wind in vain, wave-tops flashed silver against the dark rim of the world. With a feeling of infinite sadness I thought of the unconscious irony in St Columba's lines:

> *Delightful would it be to sit on the pinnacle of a rock,*
> *That I might often see the face of the ocean;*
> *That I might see its level sparkling strand,*
> *It would be no cause of sorrow . . .*

Although numbed with cold, I stood there thinking about it all, listening to the geese and watching the cloud shadows chasing each other across the moonlit sands. But now the wind was dropping and overhead a star shone brightly.

It was Christmas Day.

IX
DECEMBER THE TWENTY-SEVENTH

I woke up early that morning, long before first light. Couldn't go to sleep again, so I went down to warm my shooting stockings on the Aga and make a cuppa.

The rooks were up early, too. Just after daybreak, in their regular ritual of possession, they arrived behind the cottage to spend twenty noisy minutes squawking in their springtime trees before going off to work. Along the Latterbarrow Beck, beyond the rookery, cock pheasants crowed as they fluttered down towards fellside feeding points. Somewhere in the moss a partridge was chirping. Then the sun slanted across the shoulder of Brantrake and the valley shone icy white, shot with shafts of pale blue and Naples yellow. It was like Monet's marvellous painting of the magpie: still and clear and clean, and very beautiful.

It's seldom we have had a hard frost with a scattering of snow for the Christmas shoot, but that day was an exception. Outside the kitchen door the sharp air stabbed the lungs as fiercely as a sword-thrust and I nearly went headlong on the ice. I defrosted the windscreen, put my old labrador, Baron, to gether with my gun and a box of goodies, in the back, then slowly motored the half-mile to Knott End. As I slid gingerly round the hairpin beside the crag where the lane was thick with ice, five pheasants scuttled across from fellside woodland into the new planting. Encouraging. The planting was to be our third drive of the morning.

Bill was in the barn, setting a trestle table with sixteen pairs of knives and forks. "Morning, Hugh. What do you think of it?"

"Smashing. Girl on the box said there was a high. Have we got enough pies for lunch?"

"Plenty. Marie's going to put them in the oven during the fifth drive. I got three bottles of whisky, three dozen cans of lager and a new bottle of tomato sauce."

"I've brought some more Scotch, and some mince pies and a Christmas cake. I don't think anyone's going to feel deprived. How about the supper?"

"Game soup, steak-and-kidney pie and Christmas pud. We'll have it about half past five. Help yourself to coffee. There's some brandy in those little glasses."

"Thanks. Here's to a great day."

"Cheers."

"The birds will come off the felltop like rockets with this frost. Has Mike got the sewelling ready for the coppice drive?"

"Yes. He's going to rig it up just beforehand."

"Suppose the tarn's all frozen over?"

"Nearly two inches thick. We won't get a duck flush."

"Ducks will all be out on the river. I'd better tell the beaters we're not starting with a flush."

"They're not here yet."

"Where the hell are they?"

"All out on the booze last night. Don't worry, they'll turn up. Here's someone now."

"Little grey van. It's young Billy . . . Damn! He's brought Cruncher with him!"

"Hellfire!"

"That dog is a delinquent. When he gets a bird in his jaws you can hear the bones cracking. Oh well, just have to ask Ian to persuade Billy to keep him on a string. Where the hell is John?"

"It's probably the new Land Rover. He'll be showing it off to the lads as he collects them. Who's this coming now?"

"Big blue pick-up. It'll be the Bacon brothers."

"That's three guns confirmed. Enough to start with."

"If we ever get any beaters."

"There's the telephone. Look after things, will you? There's somebody else just come."

It's always the same on shooting days. Guns and camp followers suddenly materialise, and what with the telephone and yapping dogs and everyone chattering like monkeys, it's bedlam.

"Morning lads. Compliments of the season. Coffee for you all in the barn. There's some brandy in the little glasses . . . Yes, it is, bloody cold. It'll warm up when the sun gets over the fell . . . No, no ducks. The tarn's frozen over. Mind you, we might get one or two off the little beck in the moss – if Benny's dogs haven't been through it when he let the cows out . . . Hullo, James. Happy Christmas. We're shooting six guns plus Bill with the beaters and me at the back . . . Tommy, draw a number . . . Yes, no question, girl on the telly said there was a high. Help yourself to coffee. There's brandy in the little glasses . . . Fred, take a number . . . Cat's drinking the cream? Hell! Throw it out! . . . No you fool, throw the cat out! . . . Hullo, Edward . . . Yes, I know. Feel like that myself. Here, draw a number. We're shooting six guns. Move up two. Number from the left. We'll start as soon as we can. At the moment we've no beaters . . . No, nobody. Only Billy and Cruncher . . . Yes, I know. But it's not his fault. It was his dad's dog. Billy's looking after it . . . Yes, poor chap. He was killed last summer on the motorway . . . Oh, thank God! Here's John with the beaters . . . No, Edward, no, no, no. We'll be starting dead on time. It's all highly organised. Remember, we said nine-thirty for ten . . . What? It's five past? Oh-well, quickly then. Listen everybody. Pay attention, please. Remember, safety first. No low shots. Don't shoot any hares . . . No, there aren't any rabbits, Peter. Myxi cleaned them all out in October . . . yes, I think so, too, but I can't do anything about it . . . Yes, Fred. Shoot all the snipe you can – if you can still see them . . . No Nigel. We're not starting with a duck flush. The tarn's frozen and they're all on the river . . . Oh, all right then. Go and stand on the river bank for the first drive . . . Hey! Who are all those people out there?. . . In the lane by the entrance . . . Bunch of

Greens from up the valley? For pity's sake get them to move on. Tell them we're just starting to shoot, bang-bang, and will they please stick to the lane. Just imagine the hoo-ha if one of them got a pellet up his arse! . . . What's that? They're lost? Look, one of you, go and do some map-reading for them. Point them at the village. They'll get there by the time the boozer opens. Hullo, John. Listen, be a very good chap and get Billy to keep his dog on a string . . . Yes, he's here with Cruncher . . . Well, do your best. Remember what happened last time with that hare . . . Right, lads, let's get started . . . Mike, give Ian a hand, will you? Help him load the beaters into the trailer and get 'em off up the lane. Everybody else, this way . . .

*   *   *

I stood waiting for the drive to start. In the distance the snow-covered hump of Scawfell glimmered against a backdrop of powder-blue sky. Purple clusters of birch fringed the fellsides, branches spiky with the frost. Through stiffened clumps of rushes in the water meadows the feeder beck flowed low and clear, lighter patches of gravel marking the redds of spawning salmon. Downstream, behind me in a gap between the alders, the river flashed where it bent round below the weir. High overhead a buzzard was mewing. Then suddenly a shout from the beaters and a woodcock flickered out of the birch coppice like a little brown ghost. A few minutes later pheasants were standing on their tails above the bracken, whirring up into the bright sky . . .

*   *   *

When you stand at the back of the line you don't usually get a lot of shooting, but you do get the best. Unforgettable that day was a solitary cock pheasant I shot as it came twisting down from the felltop on set wings like an aerobatic fighter. It dropped far behind me and skidded on the frozen tarn, leaving a trail of russet and copper feathers strewn across the ice.

Don't think I'm boasting about that shot, because I'm not. Paradoxically it isn't the fast flyer that's so hard to hit. It's the slow bird hanging on the end of the gun that causes problems. With the screamer there simply isn't time to dwell on the aim, to poke. Without your thinking about it the gun comes to the shoulder in a blur of barrels, and wow! – there's the bird, dead as King Arthur, slanting down behind you. Someone shouts 'Oh, good shot!' and you puff up with pride. But in truth you haven't much idea how it happened.

* * *

In the fading light of late afternoon a faint mist spread across the valley, softening the chiaroscuro of the fells. The temperature was back again below freezing and our breath was like gunsmoke in the still air. As we stumbled home in line across the moss, ice crackling underfoot, a skein of greylags came yelping down at treetop height towards the estuary. We all crouched hopefully among the tussocks, but sixteen bodies are difficult to hide and at the last moment the geese veered sharply away. At the far end of the line Edward, to great applause, dropped one over the river.

With the exception of Cruncher who, shedding his string,

had long disappeared in pursuit of a hare, there was a certain element of competition among the dogs over this retrieve. Eventually darkness closed round us and we finished up in starlight with the distant castle clock striking five.

* * *

In the tractor shed, Mike and Bill tied birds together and hung them on a pole slung from rafters. Nailed boots clattered on the cobbles.

"What a fine bag. Let's see how many we've got . . . Twenty-seven, twenty-eight, twenty-*nine* pheasants. Marvellous! Six partridges; *eight* ducks – that's more than we expected; three woodcock; two snipe; one goose; one pigeon and a rabbit. A rabbit! That's a rare animal here. Who shot it? . . . Billy's dog caught it? Ah, well make sure Billy gets it. Hullo, what's this? A moorhen! Where the hell did that come from? . . . *My* dog caught it? Old Baron? . . . Well I'm dammed, I never saw him do it. He must have spat it out . . . Oh well, there you are. All adds to the bag . . . Result: Guns fifty, dogs two. What a great day! . . . Come on inside lads and have a slurp."

* * *

"Okay, Billy, I know you have to get back. Got your rabbit? Here, take a brace of birds for your mum. Thanks for coming. Happy New Year."

X

A MARSHLAND DROLLERY

As though impelled by magic, the tree moved slowly across the mudflats like part of Birnam Wood approaching Dunsinane. But this mysterious object, seemingly defiant of Nature's laws, was neither an animated tree nor bound for Macbeth's stronghold. It was the Falkus Walking Hide (Mk1), and in the gathering dusk of a wild November afternoon it was creeping shore-wards ahead of a flooding tide.

On close inspection, any relationship with a forest disappeared and, whatever the duck took it for, it looked to the discerning human eye exactly what it was: a ring of rigid Netlon, thatched with rushes and topped-off with sprigs of broom. This 'topping' poked up and gave the otherwise stark outline a ragged fringe, thus helping to provide a more harmless appearance. But in an attempt to make 'assurance double sure' I had draped a length of close-meshed camouflaged netting round the thatch, and it was this that gave the hide such an arboraceous look – the plastic camouflage having a curiously bark-like texture, so that when at rest the ensemble may have seemed to passing duck to be nothing but a tree stump stranded by the sea.

But whatever they thought it was, they accepted it without alarm. From it, I had come to terms with wildfowl on ground where no vestige of natural cover existed.

Apart from the birds themselves, successful wildfowling in daylight demands concealment, and if we crouch low enough we can sometimes outwit fowl from the shallowest of guts. But on the flats I was shooting, there was no gut. Not even a bed of samphire or clump of seaweed. Throughout a tidal flight, watching from the saltings, it was commonplace to see hundreds of duck fly past – all out of range.

The advent of the Walking Hide changed that picture. Now when wind and tide brought duck swinging up the creek, I was at the water's edge ready to receive them. And 'receive' them I did, because oblivious of the WH many of them obligingly flew within easy shot – as they had done on the afternoon in question, when I came in with eight wigeon, a mallard and two teal.

Most gratifying.

Carrying the hide about was no hardship. I simply rolled it up like a carpet, tied a cord round it with a slip-knot and slung it over my shoulder. The lightness of Netlon made the weight negligible. On firm ground near the flats I would unroll it, lift it upright, stand in the centre and wrap it round me. When the sticks at the two ends came together I fastened them top and bottom with pieces of string kept in place for the purpose.

To walk it about I simply bent down, grasped the meshes at knee height on either side, made sure the balance was right, then straightened up and moved off; the bottom, while on the move, being ten or twelve inches in the air.

There was a square cut out of one side at ground level. This had been replaced with a loose nylon-netting flap to let the dog in and out when he was retrieving (dead birds being hung up inside). There was just enough room for the dog when I was shooting. But walking the hide about with a labrador between my legs proved difficult; so when on the move I usually let him out.

Carrying the gun? Two courses were open. First, a cord sling that slipped over the barrels and butt. Or you could put the butt in your side pocket with the barrels leaning back against your shoulder. This worked better than the sling, since the gun was instantly ready for action if approaching birds were sighted while I was on the move, in which case I had only to push the Netlon-support-sticks into the ground, and sit down out of sight on the built-in seat – remembering always to *lean forward!*

It was the seat that made everything possible. Like that of a shooting-stick, its base was nearly as broad as its top to prevent it sinking in the mud; and fastened permanently to the hide wall, it was always ready to receive you. But great care was needed when sitting down. One's weight had to be kept well forward – rather in the position of the morning crouch. As I soon learned, failure to adopt this posture could be disastrous.

Wading across the flats in the oyster-light of dawn, and suddenly hearing the whistle of approaching wigeon, I stopped abruptly, sat down too quickly and leant back to give myself room to raise the gun . . . The next moment the sky was blotted out and I found myself flat on my back, a trickle of muddy ooze icy cold against my neck.

Helplessly encased within that Netlon cylinder, I sensed the frustration of an unhorsed French knight at Agincourt – save that no wild-eyed Welsh bowman peered down into my opened visor with dagger poised.

To re-right the hide when stretched out on one's back demanded a feat of athleticism far beyond the capability of this particular wildfowler clad in winter clobber and holding a 12-bore at full stretch above his head. Only one line of action was feasible: to roll over, crawl out on elbows and knees, scrape off the mud, stand the hide up, untie the entrance, step inside and start again. To do all this while holding a gun wasn't easy, but I managed to achieve it by dint of wedging the gun between my legs.

Apart from a readiness to capsize, the Walking Hide had no faults. It was so simple that I marvelled I hadn't tumbled to it a life-time ago. It worked just as well with mallard, or geese, or pigeon flighting to stubble. One simply walked it to whichever part of the field the birds fancied. As they changed their flight-plan, so one changed one's pitch in sympathy. All in all it was a huge success.

So – why do I write of it in the past tense?

Well, for one thing the challenge has gone. Conceived in a momentary flash of happy inspiration, it was designed as a means of shooting 'impossible' duck, something unobtrusive, that broke up the human outline but was just big enough to let me stand up and swing the gun . . . and it worked.

But I can shoot all the duck I need without it. It was just a splendid jape, a dream come true, and enormously satisfying at the time. But to persist with it just to slaughter duck would turn the fires of serendipity to ashes. Some place of sanctuary is vital to wildfowl in every estuary. It is, surely, commonsense to allow them the safety of the open tideline.

Besides, there is something else. For a lifetime, in addition to shooting wildfowl, I have fished for salmon and sea trout, because of all sporting quarries they are the most unpredictable – and so the most challenging. However cunning the lure or angling method we devise to outwit them, the chances are always in their favour; and for no reason other than the uncertainty of migratory fish behaviour, what works so well on one occasion fails dismally on another. But the Walking Hide worked every time. It was like fishing for salmon with an unfailing fly. As I proved, birds could be shot right out in the open on bare mud or sand or stubble. What had hitherto been impossible suddenly became easy, and for the first time in my life the challenge of wildfowling lost its charm.

So, I shall not use it on the marsh again. But I pass on the notion in case, just for the hell of it, any of you care to give it a fling. To keep the thing upright on mud needs practice, and I have known people defeated by it. But whether you use it yourself or watch the antics of a friend, you will find it highly entertaining.

Try it.

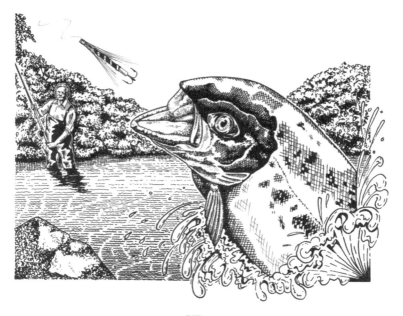

XI
BRIEF ENCOUNTER

A little while ago, reading a light-hearted book about salmon fishing by the famous footballer, Jack Charlton, who runs the Irish team, it occurred to me that a successful salmon fishing philosophy could depend on no better apprenticeship than that of a football manager.

After all, the football manager's experience, hammered out on the anvil of goal-less draws, hardens him to disappointment. Sitting glumly in his dugout he must view the antics of his unpredictable players, who leap about and do everything but score, with the same feeling of helpless frustration an angler feels when faced with a pool of leaping salmon that refuse to take.

But sometimes, suddenly, everything changes. There is a glut of goals, a plethora of hooked fish. It seems unaccountable and ridiculous. But, as I have often said, although a sense of the ridiculous is not essential to successful salmon fishing, it certainly helps.

For one thing, it conditions the mind when we are thinking of salmon and how to catch them. What is surprising about this sport is not that we catch so few salmon, but that we ever catch any at all. After all, offering something resembling food to a non-feeding fish borders on lunacy. Nevertheless, there are times when, for reasons unknown, salmon are absurdly easy to hook.

I am not suggesting that they return from sea with their brains addled. But there is no doubt that from our point of view as anglers, when salmon regain fresh water their behaviour becomes ridiculous. As A.H. Chaytor wrote in *Letters to a Salmon Fisher's Sons*:

One thing you may be sure about a salmon, you can never tell either what he will do, or when he will do it.

For me, this sense of never-being-quite-sure-what-is-going-to-happen plays a major part in the charm and excitement of salmon fishing. If this sense is ever stripped away, though the mystery of the salmon may remain, the magic of its capture will dissolve. A strange, not to say unique experience of this happened to me once on a well-known Border river.

I was one of four rods fishing a private beat for the day. The other three rods, cheery Lancashire lads I'd not met before, were fishing as a party. I was alone. What with one thing and another I was late getting away from the cottage and didn't turn up on the river until about six o'clock – just as they were heading for their 'tea' in the local.

"Hullo!" they chorused as I got out of the car. "Look who's here!"

"Any luck?" I enquired.

"No," they said. "It's hopeless. We've fished every inch of it. You'll catch nowt."

"Water looks perfect to me," I ventured.

"Oh aye," they agreed. "It is. But there's nowt in it. We started before breakfast. Flogged all day. Haven't had a touch. Coming back later for a go at the sea trout. If there *are* any!"

"May see you later, then."

"Good luck," they shouted, climbing into their Range Rover. "Hey! Hey! You'll need it!"

They drove away roaring with laughter. The thought of Falkus flogging a stretch of empty water while they were boozing happily in the pub seemed to have made their day. Thoughtfully, I set up some tackle and turned my attention to the river.

Making my way upstream, I passed a couple of long, deep pools. These I felt sure had been well hammered. Then came some faster, broken water, ideal for grilse and sea trout; a fine piece to fish on an August evening, but not what I was looking for just then. Above it, though, round a bend in the river, I came to a long, rather shallow glide where, between steep, high banks dense with trees, the water flowed steady and unbroken over a bed of firm gravel.

At a gap in the trees I stopped and stood looking at this

stretch – or what I could see of it: a comparatively narrow strip of open water hemmed in by leafy branches which hung out from either bank. About twenty yards downstream of the gap, a short run of water under the trees on the far bank attracted my attention. This possible 'taking strip', only eight or ten yards in length, had a faintly darker, more swirly look about it, as though at that point the river flowed over a slight depression, perhaps a shallow rocky trough – a perfect resting lie for running fish. The longer I gazed at it, trying to picture the river bottom at that place, the more promising it looked.

Grilse are a law unto themselves. But the fish I was hoping, indeed expecting to catch, were big fresh-run autumn salmon. Such fish, it seemed to me, would have run through the hurly-burly of the faster water downstream and, since they were not lying in the deep pools below – the Lancashire lads' experience seemed proof of that – could well have finished up in the comfortable, measured flow under those tree branches on the other bank. It *looked* right. If I were a running salmon I thought to myself, that is where I would choose to rest.

I wondered whether the lads, when fishing 'every inch' of the beat, had included the glide. I thought it unlikely. And some elementary detective work on the bankside vegetation at the gap – the only spot where it was possible to slide into the river – confirmed this view. The grass was uncrushed; there were no scuffles; no footprints. My pulses, as they say quickened. Instinctively, I began to feel that I was in with a chance.

Already my mind had been working like a computer. Should I hook a fish in those difficult conditions, I knew exactly how I would play and land it. I slid into the water, which was thigh deep against the bank, removed the lanyard from my landing net, stuck the net handle into the bankside and then tied one end of the lanyard to a tree root, leaving the other end trailing in the water. After that I waded out waist deep to the end of the tree branches and made my way carefully downstream.

On the other bank, under the trees, not far above my assumed taking strip, lodged among the tree roots by some recent spate, was a white plastic fertiliser bag. Usually I view such unsightly objects with regret. But in this case I welcomed it. It made an excellent casting marker: a point to aim at.

The water in that short taking strip where I thought the fish were lying, was I reckoned, between five and six feet deep. I wanted my fly to fish about two feet off the bottom. That to me is the ideal presentation depth for sunk line fishing in cold water.

Yes, I know that salmon in these conditions will sometimes come up and take a fly on or just under the surface. I've caught them there. Sometimes. But most of the time, for my money, the fly fishes deep. I'm not talking about 'scraping the bottom', that's nonsense. A few inches above the fishes' noses is where I want the fly to pass. And to me, a fly that is fishing four feet down in six feet of water is 'deep'.

When I was within casting range of the white marker I stripped off sufficient line and let it drift with the fly straight downstream, sinking as it went. Then, with both wrists, I rolled it to the surface, whisked it back upstream into a figure-of-eight loop and, with a tilted rod, Spey cast it towards the opposite bank.

I call this cast the 'square-cut' – that beautiful and deeply satisfying stroke wide of point, remembered from my cricketing days. The sight of the line snaking out a foot or so above the water, then curling in under the branches so that the fly plopped down close to the white bag, filled me with delight.

There was an interval of breathless anticipation, lasting perhaps five or six seconds, as the fly sank and swung round under the branches . . . Then suddenly – wow!

As usual when a salmon takes there was nothing dramatic. With a tightening of the line the fly just stopped, as though caught in the bottom. I raised the rod – and there he was! A big fellow, lugging away on the line almost as though in slow motion.

What was so wonderful about that particular take was the realisation that my water sense had won an Oscar. But of course, as always when a salmon takes my fly, I experienced the three intense emotions of disbelief, magic and jubilation, fused into a single moment of triumph.

But in the present situation there was no time to dwell on self-praise. If a fish of that size ran downstream there was no chance of following him. I had to walk him upstream, as I had planned to do, and land him at the gap. Immediately I turned sideways-on to the current and, with my rod held at right-angles to the river, waded steadily back upstream to the gap in the trees.

The fish followed faithfully, like a dog. (A 'walked' fish will nearly always come with you if taken in hand soon enough.) But when I reached the gap I stopped. And the fish, as I expected, suddenly woke up. This was the place where I had already decided to fight and land a fish. There was no question of letting him run far. He had to be landed on the spot. I was, of course, using immensely strong tackle.

As always, every item had been tested before I started fishing. The fly-line stripped off the reel and re-wound evenly and firmly. The leader was a yard or so of new sea-fishing nylon that would have held a shark. The treble hook in the two-inch plain black and orange tube could have balanced a coal bucket (it had when I originally tested it). There was plenty of backing. All knots had been carefully tied and from experience were the best I knew. In my philosophy there are many reasons but very few excuses for being broken – the angler's ultimate disgrace. Usually it is due to lack of attention to detail. Well, nobody could accuse me of that.

Apart from avoiding being broken, I use such strong tackle to reduce playing time to a minimum. Therefore, if I choose to release a fish, I can do so without its having suffered unduly.

The fish I'd hooked was upwards of twenty pounds I reckoned, but I gave not an inch of ground. He rushed off across the river like a torpedo and ran upstream under the trees. This was just what I wanted. He slowed down and stopped after about thirty yards, whereupon I lowered the rod and holding it sideways to the fish put a finger on the reel and pulled. A few seconds of this leverage turned the fish so that he swung round and, still heading obliquely upstream, charged across to my own bank. Now, from my point of view, he was in the best possible position. I quickly wound up the slack line I had stripped in when he'd come across, and applied maximum pressure. The longer you take (and most people take far too long), the more time he has to shed the hook. If I gave this fish too much stick and the hook pulled through its hold, well let it. Whatever happened, pusillanimity was not going to be responsible for losing him.

Relying on the strength of my terminal tackle, I kept pulling his head downstream. The net handle was gripped between my legs and as the fish swung out from underneath the branches, I ignored the plunging and kicking and dragged him straight back across the rim. I raised the net – and there he was, a great big cock fish folded up inside and splashing madly, but mine!

I stuffed the rod butt down inside my breast waders and killed the fish with the priest hanging round my neck.

This was the most difficult part of the proceedings, achieved by jamming the net's rim against the bank and so, with the handle clamped between my thighs, giving myself the use of both hands. From start to finish the fish had taken only a few minutes to land simply because, never having seen me, he had remained unscared. Puzzled maybe, but not frightened – the most important aspect of any quick landing. Invisible against the loom of the bank, I had kept out of sight the whole time.

After that it was easy. I removed the hook, and threaded the loose end of the net cord – which I had previously tied to the tree root – through the fish's gills. Then, letting the dead fish wave gently in the current, I tied the cord back on the root alongside the original knot.

* * *

Fifty minutes later I was standing in the same place, but now there were *five* big salmon trailing side by side on the net lanyard in the streamy water below that tree root. Four more casts

I had made towards the plastic bag, and each cast had rung up the three roses.

At last the scales had fallen from my eyes. Clearly this was one of those rare occasions when I had managed to sneak in and catch Fate off her guard. Usually, as most salmon fishers know to their cost, one arrives on location only to be told that conditions were very good yesterday and will probably be even better tomorrow; but, 'chidden by God,' are fuck-all good today. Well, for me, today was perfect for that lie under the branches. Almost certainly it was only a very temporary resting place, whose tenancy depended on an exact height (and probably temperature), of water. A shoal of big fish lying there today. No fish lying there tomorrow – they'd have run during the night.

Quite possibly there hadn't been a single fish lying there all season, and there mightn't be another before the season's end. For once, old Falkus had hit the jackpot.

*   *   *

By now the setting sun was a dull blush in the clouds and most of the river had dissolved into shadow. Quite suddenly it seemed, the current gurgling underneath the far branches had become black and mysterious. Between the tree-lined banks I had the sensation of wading in a tunnel, casting across jigsaw patches of light and shade into a distant crevice of darkness.

For the sixth time, aimed at the white plastic bag, my fly curled under the branches, sank and swung round. And for the sixth time, in the same place as before, dead on cue – it stopped.

For the sixth time I went through the, by now, familiar routine. But, as I walked the gently lugging fish upstream towards the gap, I realised that there was no longer the excitement. It was all too easy. It had indeed become, simply, a routine . . .

This time, as I drew the tiring fish in towards the net I could see that it wasn't well hooked. A big hen fish, it turned broadside-on and hung there in the current just short of the net. The hook was plainly visible, fastened only by a sliver of skin. The fish was tantalisingly close, but for me to pull harder could only court disaster. To allow the fish more freedom seemed equally futile. A second or two later however, our impasse was ended as the wisp of skin broke free. For a moment or two the fish dropped back sideways with the stream, then with a flick of its tail, it swung round in a flash of silver and was gone.

To lose a big fish is always a wrench, but I honestly didn't regret the loss of that fish. It was the one female I'd hooked, and even in that moment of frustration I'd known I would have freed her unharmed.

Conscious that I was going to miss the best hour of the day, I cut off the fly, put it away and wound in the line. I didn't want to wade down that strip of water again. I knew that if I put out another cast towards that plastic bag I should hook another fish. I *knew*. And suddenly I didn't want to do it. I had hooked six fish in six casts, landing five averaging over twenty pounds. What more was there left to prove? There would be smoked salmon for all my friends at Christmas. I'd caught enough. Losing that fish had sealed the issue. It was time to stop.

Of course, had the spirit moved me, I could have gone on fishing and played at catch-and-release. But to do that purposely is to change angling from a sport into a game, and that is something I could never do.

I pitched the landing net up on top of the bank, threw the wading staff after it, and then the rod. With the river curling round my thighs I stood where I was for a little while, thinking about it all.

Quite apart from the size of the fish, it had been a strange experience, almost uncanny. But there was no witchcraft wound up in the way those fish were caught. Success had hung on two things: water sense and good casting. I looked across the darkening river to the white plastic bag that glimmered faintly in the dusk. Anyone who could have Spey cast a sinking line and put the fly under those tree branches would have done just as well as I had. It was an example of why casting ability is sometimes the key factor in hooking salmon. If I hadn't been able to make that particular type of Spey cast, I'd have caught nothing. It was as simple as that.

I crawled up the bank and, with great difficulty, hauled the fish up after me. Then, looking like the Ancient Mariner with his albatross, I slung them round my neck and lugged them back to the car. By the time I got there I must have felt worse than he did. Even an albatross doesn't weigh a hundredweight!

No sooner had I got the fish packed into the boot, and settled myself thankfully into the driving seat, when back from the pub came the wedding . . . sorry, the fishing guests.

"Ah, there he is!" they chorused. "The man himself! Look! He's packing up!" They disentangled themselves from their seat-belts and staggered across. "Had enough of it, then?"

"Yes," I said. "I've had enough."

"We told you so," they crowed. "Ha! Ha! Ha! We told you there was nowt in the river."

"You did," I agreed, starting the car. "You certainly did. All the same, if I were you, I'd try that reach upstream between the trees before it gets too dark. It looks promising."

"No," they demurred. "It's all grown up, you can't fish it. Anyway it wouldn't be worthwhile, there's nothing come in."

"Never you mind," said one of them consolingly. "Even you can't catch what isn't there."

"That's very true," I said. "Well – good luck, lads." I let in the clutch and drove away into the darkening, leaving them there chortling with glee at the thought of the big-headed old bugger getting his come-uppance.

* * *

Late that night the fishery manager rang me to find out how I'd got on. I told him.

"Good God!" he said. "I heard you'd packed up early and caught nothing. What happened, did the fish just stop taking?"

"No," I said. "I just stopped fishing."

"You *stopped*?" he exclaimed incredulously. "In the middle of it all? You don't expect me to believe that, do you?"

"No," I said. "I suppose I don't really. But that's what happened."

There was a silence. Then:

"Hey, listen," he burst out. "The other rods told me they fished all day long. They're experienced anglers. Nobody had a touch. You're having me on."

I put him right about that, and finally convinced him I really had caught some fish, but pointed out that the whole thing had simply got out of hand. For once, quite by chance, Nature had been turned upside-down. There was no longer any challenge. I'd had a fish with every cast and the magic had gone.

I went on like this for some time, trying to explain why, at the peak of success – during a season when so little had been caught – I'd stopped fishing. But he still didn't seem to understand.

XII
CHAYTOR

To any salmon fly fishers who feel deprived of success, the best advice I can offer is to read A.H. Chaytor's *Letters to a Salmon Fisher's Sons*. Published in 1910, this is a classic piece of angling literature. But be warned – it is a very uneven book. The illustrations are meagre. There are some long, unparagraphed slabs of text which describe in tedious detail what a few simple diagrams could explain more clearly in a fraction of the space. To the modern angler, much of the material dealing with salmon spawning and hatching, Edwardian tackle, ferreting and various other odds-and-ends is of scant interest, and the use of the gaff strikes a discordant note. So, why should anyone find it worthwhile to wade through *Letters to a Salmon Fisher's Sons*? At a glance it seems strange that this book should claim the right to be termed a 'classic'. Yet, for all its shortcomings, make no mistake, a classic it most certainly is.

Chaytor was a barrister and some of his writing is tinged with a lawyer's dryness, but shining through it is not only an immense enthusiasm for the sport of salmon fishing, and the instincts of a genuine sportsman, but the acuity and originality of his observations. Despite the huge amount of advice issuing from the angling press of today, few, if any, salmon fishers, whatever their experience, could fail to profit from these pages. Chaytor should be read partly from curiosity and partly for his descriptive writing; but most of all because in contrast to the majority of latterday scribes – much of whose material is based on prejudice, conjecture and superstition – he writes with such crashing down-to-earth *commonsense*.

Here he is on the highly vexed subject of wading and angling safety. Written nearly a hundred years ago, the advice is original and utterly sound:

Great controversy rages in the smoking rooms of fishing inns as to whether you should or should not wear a strap round your waist when wading in dangerous waters. Many anglers assert that . . . the buoyancy of your legs will drown you by causing your head to go under water and your feet to bob about on the surface like corks. I have even met men who vowed that they had seen this happen. Well, that is all utter nonsense . . . I have tried it more than once by deliberately upsetting out of a boat when crossing the river in my waders, and the result is nothing of the sort. The buoyancy is enough to keep your legs well up, but it does not bother you at all, and you swim quite easily.

Chaytor, however sophisticated his profession, was a boy at heart with unlimited enthusiasms of boyhood which, if we are lucky, are never lost. In that respect he was certainly blessed:

You are fishing for spring salmon in a time of hope and joy, and of budding leaves and singing birds, and at the beginning of a new salmon season when the mere casting of the fly again is a perfect holiday . . . The very thought of a rod and a salmon pool can make me feel like a schoolboy going home for the holidays.

A holiday angler he may chiefly have been, but from his writing it is abundantly clear what he would have thought about the modern 'weekend experts' whose parrottings in the press have become so familiar in recent years. Coming as many of them do from the reservoirs, they could benefit from reading Chaytor's comments:

We most of us begin as trout fishers, and after a season or two of salmon fishing we feel that we know all about it . . . But a larger experience brings doubts. We find that in low waters and in the worst conditions some few men can regularly catch fish, whilst everybody else on the river is doing nothing. When salmon are taking freely almost anyone who can throw a fly may catch a salmon, but at other times the difference between a really good and merely ordinary fisher is just as great in salmon fishing as it is between the good and the ordinary performer in every other sport.

And there is little doubt that for Chaytor the difference in skill was measured in terms of fly fishing – as his thoughts on sportsmanship make clear:

People will ask why do you so greatly prefer fly fishing, and think poorly even of artificial minnow fishing, and rather despise the pleasures of prawn and worm and any natural bait. Well, it comes to a personal matter of taste and of one's own education in sport . . . We have all been pot-hunters at times, and with salmon the temptation is all the greater as they are here today and gone tomorrow, and in the meanwhile they jump out under our noses and excite our keen desire and refuse our flies for days or weeks together. But when I do catch such a salmon with a prawn I feel rather a poacher and can't take any pride in it, as I should do if I had tempted him to take a fly.

When it comes to the practical 'what to do?' approach to salmon fishing, Chaytor offers some of the best advice ever written:

One thing you may be sure of about a salmon, you can never tell either what he will do, or when he will do it, and if the fish doesn't come when invited in what you consider the orthodox manner, don't give him up, but try him in the most unorthodox way that you can think of, and I should suggest, to begin with, an absurdly small fly.

He was indeed a great simplifier. Much has been written about the effect on salmon behaviour of wind, air temperature and light. Chaytor has little to do with it:

Cold winds and wretched weather, which send the trout fisher home empty-handed, seem often to make little or no difference to the salmon. The wind and the weather do affect success in salmon fishing, but in a very uncertain and capricious manner . . . No day and no weather is hopeless if there are salmon in the pools . . . If the air is clear and without mist the day may be as hot or as cold, as sunny or as dark as you will, and still you may have a very fine day's salmon fishing.

On the subject of where and when to expect salmon he is particularly good – voicing, as usual, an original thought:

There are – or one gets to believe that there are – certain times of the day which seem to be critical times, when salmon take, if they are going to take at all . . . and of them all I should put dusk first . . . Many and many a time I have known two, three, and four fish to be taken in this hour by a rod that had moved nothing all day. But too often the fisher had gone home to dinner at the very time when he should be fishing the hardest. The best chance lasts but a short time and comes after sunset, when the light has failed so much that the surface of the water seems to reflect it all, and you seem to be casting into a river of liquid metal . . . Keep one of your likeliest spots for the last few casts in the failing light, and be careful to disturb the fish there as little as possible during the afternoon.

That advice cannot be bettered. Again, on the subject of night fishing for salmon, he is ahead of the field:

*When it has grown quite dark, you may use your very largest fly,
and may take fish that would not look at anything during the day.*

In the face of general scepticism I have proved the truth of
this observation when night fishing with my big Sunk Lure on
many different rivers.

Chaytor wrote his book in the form of letters to his sons and
concerns himself chiefly with advice on catching salmon. I
write 'on *catching* salmon' advisedly because notwithstanding
his dedication to the fly, he was a highly successful fish *catcher*.
Reading him, I get the feeling that if a pool held a taking fish,
Chaytor was the chap to winkle it out when other rods had
failed. This proclivity is very uncommon. I have known many
experienced salmon fishers, competent casters and intelligent in
their approach, but whose success rate never rose above the
average, whereas a few, a very few, have had the uncanny knack
of invariably being top rod. Chaytor was in the same class.

Drewett Chaytor wrote of his father:

*His success, measured by the takes of others on the same river, was
often remarkable. It was particularly noticeable in difficult conditions such as dead low water, that he seemed always to be able to
catch fish when few others could do so.*

Perhaps, after we have read and digested some of his excellent
advice, we may find the consistency of his catches less astonishing. Certainly he himself was never lured by the mirage of
success:

Of the pleasure of success in fishing I need say nothing. We all know it; and we have all felt it . . . But even success has its limits; the fish is caught, the thing is done. It is our lost fish that I believe stay longest in our memory, and seize upon our thoughts whenever we look back to fishing days . . . the fish that has beaten us and left us quivering with excitement and vexation, is hooked and lost again in many a year to come.

And there let us leave him, writing his letters – often in a carriage on the express train London-bound from his beloved salmon beat below Hexham on the River Tyne. Later, to the thunderous accompaniment of heavy guns, he was to write part of a second edition within his billet amid the horrors of Flanders in 1915-16, prior to the gas attack that rendered him an invalid and virtually ended his fishing.

If Fate could give me the chance of spending a day with any salmon fisher of the past, I think I would choose Chaytor. It would be an education to watch him at work, teasing one out of the pool in dead low water after everyone else had given it best.

Chaytor, sportsman *par excellence*. His commonsense approach to salmon fishing has been an inspiration to generations of anglers. As indeed, it has to me.

XIII
THE WOMAN AND THE FISH

During the 1920s, women anglers established three astonishing British salmon records that have not been beaten.

From the Tay in October 1922, Miss Georgina Ballantine landed a fish of 64lb. The biggest ever caught on rod and line. From the Deveron in October, 1924, Mrs Clementina Morrison landed the fly-caught record: a 61-pounder. From the Wye in 1923, Miss Doreen Davey caught the record spring fish of 59½lb. In that decade, British rivers provided women anglers with at least two other exceptional fish: a 55-pounder by Mrs Gladys Huntington from the Awe on 19th September, 1927, and a 50-pounder from the Tay at Kinnaird by Miss Lettice Ward on 12th October, 1932.

At the time, the capture of these monsters aroused a lot of

interest. What seemed extraordinary then (and still does) was that such a tiny minority of women salmon fishers could account for so many of the biggest fish landed.

Their success during the Thirties continued to surprise. Fishing the Tweed for a day in 1935, Lady Joan Joicey made the remarkable catch of twenty-six salmon and two sea trout. It was merely one among many notable bags by women anglers, achieved while 'Jock Scott' (the pen-name of D.L. Rudd) was preparing the manuscript of his book: *Game Fish Records* (H.F. & G. Witherby, 1936). Puzzled by the statistics, he wrote:

> *I have often wondered why ladies prove to be so exceptionally successful at salmon fishing. The luring of 60-pounders appears to be a lost art amongst male anglers in the British Isles, or can it be that ultra-large salmon prefer being caught by ladies?* Quien sabe? *Whatever secret feminine anglers possess, it is, judging by results, a very potent one, and I wish I could discover it!*

Unwittingly, 'Jock Scott' may have stumbled on an astonishing possibility: that there really was a secret. Although most people in the angling world would be prepared to attribute women's success either to luck or skill, or both, there may be yet another cause. First, the scientific.

Prompted by an hypothesis relating to feeding and non-feeding mechanisms of the salmon suggested by my friend Dr David Goldsborough and published in my book *Salmon Fishing* (H.F. & G. Witherby, 1984), another of my fishing friends, Professor Peter Behan of Glasgow University, has been researching anorexia in fish – a not uncommon starvation syndrome which affects humans and can be fatal. During the course of his experiments, he became deeply interested in the salmon's amazing capacity to smell and taste, those remarkable senses that guide a fish back from the sea to its natal river. Was it possible that the big male salmon often caught by women at the back-end of the season could actually sense the stimulating proximity of a female angler?

Social communication among fish – controlling dominance, sexual behaviour and aggression – is achieved through the chemical messages of pheromones: substances given off in scent, usually from the skin, which can affect the behaviour of other animals not necessarily of the same species. It is known that salmon can detect water-borne chemical messages to an astonishing degree. For instance, the odours of a man's hand will sometimes repel or alarm salmon, whereas those of a women's hand will not. A first-hand account of this phenomenon (no pun intended) comes from Mr Garry Hewitt of Lewiston, Idaho, USA:

When I heard about this I finally understood something that occurred on the Clearwater River, Idaho, back in 1966. The man counting the fish passing the Portlatch Dam claimed that he could stop salmon and steelhead trout from entering the dam's fish ladder by merely putting one finger into the water at the top of the ladder. He said he didn't like to do this very often because it would keep fish out of the ladder for as long as thirty minutes, delaying fish passage.

One day when friends and I were visiting the dam, just as the fish counter was about to demonstrate his finger trick, the only woman in our group volunteered to do it.

When she put her finger into the water at the head of the ladder, upstream from the observation window, the fish continued to swim past the window without a sign of agitation. The fish counter told her to put her entire hand into the water and swish it back and forth. She did this for about a minute. The fish took no notice.

Then the fish counter went to the head of the ladder, to the same place where the woman was, put one finger into the water and for about ten seconds swished it to and fro. A few seconds later the fish in the observation window became extremely agitated. Then they turned tail and swam back down the ladder.

At that, all of us went up on top where we could observe the lower part of the ladder. All over the place downstream, fish were jumping out of the water seemingly in panic.

The fish counter had no explanation why the woman's hand hadn't frightened the fish. Of course, at that time no one knew anything about chemical communication.

Today I always wash my hands before going fishing. I even wash before a session of fly-tying to keep my flies 'uncontaminated'. When I do this I find that I can catch trout almost as well as my wife!

That salmon might respond to women via the female pheromones is a theory yet to be proved, but some scientists think it not unlikely. To quote the famous Norwegian biologist, Professor Doving:

It is quite possible that salmon can sense the sex hormones of women and become attracted to them, even if these come in minute quantities on an angling lure.

* * *

A further line of enquiry is a discussion with a large number of successful female anglers about their methods and opinions. By many of the ladies interviewed, the suggestion that there could be a scientific explanation of their success was greeted with scepticism and amusement. Some thought it a conspiracy of male chauvinists, bad losers to a man, who were prepared to attribute female superiority in a predominantly masculine sport to a form of witchcraft rather than to skill and dedication.

But what, non-salmon-fishing readers may reasonably ask, is so remarkable about catching salmon either big or small? Why so much fuss? For their benefit, I should explain that salmon are migratory fish. They are born and spend the first couple of years or so of their lives in the fresh water of a river, after which they go to sea, feed avidly for a period varying between one and three or four years, then return to the river as adults to mate and spawn. But what makes the sport of salmon fishing so special is that on their return from the sea salmon *stop feeding*. A casual onlooker, therefore, might be forgiven for regarding the hooking of this fish as an esoteric rite, in which sorcery must of necessity play a major part.

Extraordinary though it may be, however, although the returning salmon take no further food they will sometimes, inexplicably, take an angler's bait or lure. Why? Nobody knows. Many hypotheses have been advanced but none has been proved. Small wonder then that, to an outsider, anyone fishing for salmon with rod and line must be slightly deranged.

After all, who but a simpleton would expect to hook a fish that, while lying in the river waiting to spawn, has no appetite, lives on the supply of nourishment stored in its tissues and has no need of food? What is surprising is not that salmon are hard to catch, but that any are caught at all. Why should this non-feeding fish ever take any sort of bait or lure?

And of course during most of the time we cast to them, they won't take. Salmon frequently seem impossible to catch. They just lie there, refusing everything on offer – until, suddenly, one of them will treat our offering like a long-awaited snack and half-swallow it. Or – as if this behaviour were not by itself sufficiently surprising and illogical – a fish will suck the thing in and puff it out again, or tweak it, or chin it, or slap it with his tail, or roll on it (if it's lying on the bottom), or half-take it, stand-on-end and balance it on his nose. I have watched salmon do all of these things.

It is an axiom of hunters that to be successful they must learn to think like the creatures they hunt. When salmon are the quarry, the humourist who said: 'You don't have to be crazy to go fishing, but it helps,' was nearer the truth than he probably imagined. The salmon is a crazy fish and to excel as a salmon angler one has to be, if not raving, at least shall we say infinitely flexible in one's approach.

Is it surprising, then, that the success rate of women is so high? They are, after all, built on rather different lines from men.

Don't misunderstand me. Not for one moment am I implying that female anglers are madder than male anglers, merely that they have a different way of seeing things. They are, I suggest, more capable of adapting to crazy situations. Once seized with the lust for salmon they will fish with utter determination – especially if there are men fishing the water too. Nothing diminishes their concentration. Foul weather will not discourage them, nor physical discomfort quench their spirit. Whatever the chances, they will stick it out, refusing to be beaten, and I have known only darkness drive them from the river. Years ago, in my film; *Salmo the Leaper*, following a sequence when my host's wife comes in with two fish to my one, I wrote:

Often enough the women will beat the men . . . I put it down to their sheer dogged persistence. Once they start fishing they simply will not give up.

You think I exaggerate? Listen. Have you ever tried sharing a rod with a woman for a day on a salmon beat? I have. I spent the first half-hour teaching her the rudiments of Spey casting – and the rest of the day gillying. Take my advice, if you want to do any fishing yourself *always* arrange for two rods. Once her claws curl round that cork grip you will never get it back. Sharing is over for the day . . . (What's that? . . . You must be joking. Just you try prising those fingers loose. Whisking round the house with vacuum cleaners gives women very strong wrists – one reason why they make such good Spey casters.)

Just in case you think I'm going adrift in my old age, let me assure you that if my life were at stake I would fish for salmon against anybody, male or female; but if Fate demanded a team match, I would unhesitatingly choose a team of women.

Years of teaching salmon fishing and Spey casting have convinced me that a lot of men – successful businessmen in particular – just hate the idea of having lessons. Even the thought of 'going back to school' is anathema (although, my word! from what I see on my travels they could profit from some casting tuition!). Women, on the other hand, seek good advice and usually act on it. Mr Eddie McCarthy, Fishery Superintendent of the River Thurso, is very interesting on this point:

Women are much more attentive and ninety per cent easier to teach than men. What's more, they retain what they have been taught better than men do. Women have a very strong competitive spirit and they want to outdo the men, probably because as anglers most men don't take them seriously . . . Men can be very rude about lady fishers behind their backs, you should hear them in the bar! But the ladies are consistently successful, and there was one week in particular on the Thurso, in April 1987, which is memorable. Twenty-six by the ladies of the party and only two by the men. And those were on the Saturday!

After all this it comes as no surprise to find that the first angling book printed in English, *A Treatyse of Fysshynge with an Angle,* is attributed to a woman: Dame Juliana Berners. Published in 1496, after the manuscript had been copied by monks in 1450, it was probably written circa 1425. And a very good book it is. Yes, I know, the feminine authorship has been pooh-poohed. But not by me. Having studied the book I am a firm believer in Dame Juliana. And indeed, why not? Women can do it today. Why not then?

There have been many women who could fish as well as any men and better than most. That their exploits have not received more publicity may be due simply to male chauvinism. The King of Fish represents the pinnacle of many a man's hunting prowess. There is, perhaps, something atavistic in his desire to prove his manhood, proudly to exhibit the spoils of the chase to an admiring wife and family – as many cave paintings and drawings suggest has been done since human time began. Besides, some examples come from the years during two world wars, when there was scant news space for details of wealthy women angling in safe luxury on remote northern rivers.

It must not be thought, however, that tales of feminine success belong only to the distant past. Here is a note from my old mate Arthur Oglesby:

Concerning your quest to relate the capture of big salmon to the female species. In Norway, on the opening day of the 1984 season, Toril Haraldsen was fishing the Vosso. She started at around 10am and packed up just before dinner. During that time she hooked and landed ten salmon averaging 37lb. The biggest went to 53lb! It was considered to be the most noteworthy catch I have ever heard about by a woman – or a man for that matter.

Another intriguing first-hand account comes from Asbjorn Fiva, one of Norway's finest all round fly fishers and sportsmen. Raised on the banks of the Rauma River in the beautiful Romsdal valley, he was an expert salmon fisher by the age of fifteen and worked for some years as a gillie on the superb Bromley Davenport water. Among regular visitors to the river was a couple from Oslo. Invariably, both in size and number, the wife's catch of salmon was bigger than her husband's. When it was suggested to Asbjorn recently that this may have been due to the lady's pheromones, he replied:

I like your English humour, but I can easily tell you why the lady always caught more fish than the gentlemen: it was because she always did everything I tell her. She put on the fly that I advised, she cast the fly in the place I suggested, and if I suggested something else she did it without question. You see, I know my river. I know all the lies where the fish take. All she had to do was to cover them correctly. The gentleman was too clever an angler, too proud to accept advice. He followed his own ideas and caught little or nothing. If there were fish in the river, the lady caught them.

The ability of women to beat the men on the same day in the same water occurs time and again. The following example appeared in an article for *Country Life*, by that keen sportsman Max Hastings, former editor of *The Daily Telegraph*:

Women, when they choose, are often better fishers than men – perhaps they possess a more highly developed sense of rhythm. But I suspect that many take up a rod only in self-defence, in order to make the best of it when their husbands insist upon an annual migration to Scotland . . . My own wife will happily cast a fly if we are together on a salmon river, and a year or two ago much enjoyed hooking two salmon in ten minutes on a day that I could do nothing.

I do not think she would regard it as a great deprivation if she was told that she could never fish again. But it is infinitely agreeable for any woman to demonstrate that, when she chooses, she can wipe the eye of lesser (male) mortals. Among Barbara Cartland's many qualities, determination and courage rank high. There was a story of her on the Helmsdale a few years ago, mercilessly teasing the men in her party every evening in the lodge about their inability to catch fish in bright sunshine and low water.

One of them, supremely provoked, was rash enough to mutter something about: 'Well, I'd like to see you do any better.' The next morning, the pink Rolls-Royce bore the prodigious novelist majestically to the riverside. A few casts later, she hooked her fish. Ten minutes on, the triumphant procession returned in state to the lodge, having made its point. That is show business for you.

It certainly is. But more, much more than that is Barbara Cartland's sublime display of confidence. The biology of the salmon being what it is, she was on a beating to nothing. But she triumphed. In salmon fishing, absolute confidence is probably the most important asset of all.

Even so, it should be remembered that a salmon's power of scent is almost incredibly acute and that although Peter Behan's vital chemical which may attract the salmon has not yet been isolated, there might, just, be something in it. Fishing literature abounds with accounts of salmon and women that border on the supernatural.

I am reminded of the extraordinary story of a children's nanny who accompanied her employers on a week's fishing trip to Ireland. By the Friday afternoon the three anglers in the party, all male, had caught nothing. For a bit of fun, Nanny, who had never fished before, was offered a rod and invited to 'have a go'. She accepted and, after half-an-hour's roll-casting instruction, waded in and launched her fly. A salmon took it at once.

Evoking mixed family feelings of chagrin and delight, this

fish was quickly followed by another . . . and yet another.

The next morning, with an hour or so to spare before they left for home, Nanny went in again – and caught two more.

Final score: Nanny 5, The Rest 0.

Of course, all this proves nothing. But it's interesting, huh?

XIV

THE SEA TROUT

The big fish was lying above a rock at the head of the pool. Coming carelessly to the bank, I caught a lucky glimpse of him and stopped just in time, sinking slowly on hands and knees among the broom.

At full length I inched my way through long grass to the pool's edge and peered over. The fish was still there. A huge, grey shadow; so big that, at first sight, it seemed certain he must be a salmon. Then, through a clear 'window' in the flickering current, I saw his tail – the unmistakable convex tail – and gasped in astonishment. He was unquestionably a sea trout. An enormous sea trout. The biggest sea trout I had ever seen.

I lay motionless, gazing at the fish, and the sun burned hot on my back. A high June day with a warm scent of damp hay;

179

the valley steaming after early rain. Since dawn the spate had fallen quickly. Those foaming white streamers which earlier had ribboned the fellside were gone, and now in mid-afternoon the river had lost its tinge of colour and was running clear again over the pale stones.

Down towards the pool tail between shallows and deeps was the newly arrived sea trout shoal: a host of shadows, faint and grey and still. And with them from the distant seaway had come the great fish that lay in front of me. On the night tide he had nosed his way into the estuary, tasting the thin water of his homecoming and running on upstream as a spate foamed over the shallows above the weir.

He lay steady as a log, a few yards out from the bank in four or five feet of streamy water, broad tail gently waving; a round, white lamprey scar showing clearly on his flank just above the anal fin. Suddenly, he turned on his side and made a short dart upstream, low against the bottom. The river flashed silver and I caught my breath at the sheer size of him. Three feet of silver and lilac beauty, humped with strength; his weight, well into the teens of pounds. He dropped slowly back again, tail first, into his original lie.

I gazed with wistful longing at that astonishing fish, every predatory instinct quivering with excitement and desire. The sea trout of my dreams – hanging like the fruit of Tantalus a few yards from me. I might as well wish the moon as hope to catch him. And yet . . .

The river was falling fast. How long would he lie there? Half a day and a night, perhaps. By next daybreak he could have run, or dropped back to deeper water under the alder roots. I resisted a sudden temptation to hurry to the cottage for a rod. There was little hope of hooking him in that crystal sunlit water. My best chance, probably my only chance, would be that evening when the light had gone and dusk shadowed the pool. Wiser to leave him undisturbed till then.

Eight hours to sunset. I glanced at the sky. No sign of further rain. Good. If the weather held; if the fish kept to his lie; if I curbed an impatience to cast for him too soon, and waited until the magic moment of late dusk – *then*, if my fly were to flicker temptingly past his nose there was a chance, just a chance he might take.

Slowly, a picture of his life burned into my mind: the depth of water, the set and strength of current, the exact place on the opposite bank from which to cast, the length of line needed to cover him.

I wriggled backwards out of the bushes and pushed myself up on clenched fists, knuckles laced with the jigsaw pattern of damp grass. Every sense tingled at the thought of catching that fish. I longed to hook him; to feel his strength. To fight it out in the darkness.

* * *

It was a windless dusk, the tree-tops a silent tracery of leaves against the evening star. I sat under a high sycamore in the lengthening shadows, watching the river, thinking of my big fish and wondering whether he was still in residence. It seemed probable that he was. My companions were fishing only the lower pools, and no one had disturbed him.

With the fading light, a chill came into the air. The sky was full of stars, and a wreath of ground mist hung low over the water meadows. I rubbed my silk-dressed line free of grease and left fifteen yards together with leader and fly to soak in a pool among the rocks.

Ten minutes to midnight. I had waited hopefully for a cloud to soften the starlit sky, but now a faint glow was beginning to spread above the eastern fells. Soon, bright moonlight would shine straight down the pool, and I realised I could afford to wait no longer. It was time to start.

I wound up the slack line, tested hook point and knots, and walked softly up the shingle to the pool neck.

The river was shadowy and mysterious. Arcturus, the night fisherman's star, flashed above the trees, its reflection shaking in the water at my feet. Wading carefully in, well above the big sea trout's lie, I made a few practice casts to ensure that line and fly were sinking. Then, moving a yard or two downstream, I cast again, feeling the slow drag of the line as it swung round, the slight tug of the water at my fly. Two more long paces brought me to the spot I had marked that afternoon. My next cast, or the one following, should cover the fish.

I paused, heart thumping, filled with a tingling anticipation. This was it. This was the moment. *Now* – have at him, and, God! Let it be a good cast. The line sang in the air and went out into the bushy darkness under the opposite bank.

The fly seemed scarcely to touch the water. No sooner had it started to swing than I felt the line tighten with a slow, heavy pull . . .

Hardly had I realised he was hooked when the fish was on the surface, slashing in a ring of foam. A moment later the reel screamed as he went zooming off like a torpedo down the pool.

I stumbled desperately to the shore and began to run downstream along the shingle. A flurry of spray gleamed in the darkness at the pool tail, then the fish was over the lip and away down the glide beyond.

To follow him along the thickly wooded bank was impossible. I plunged on into the river beyond the shingle and splashed downstream in pursuit. Still the reel screamed. Would the fish never stop? Water surged in over my waders and clutched at my stomach. I had an unhappy feeling there was very little backing left on the reel.

Now the water was chest high and I was holding the rod at arm's length above my head. I put a finger on the reel drum. The backing was almost gone. I hung on as the rod bent and bent, and the line hummed taut.

And then, everything went slack.

I stood, numb with disappointment, water lapping my chest, the line hanging from the rod in a limp curve.

Sadly, filled with the bitterness of failure, I started to reel in.

Suddenly, the line tightened with a jerk that nearly pulled the rod from my hand. My heart leaped. There was a thumping great splosh somewhere far below me in the darkness under the alders, then again the line went slack – as, for a second time, the fish turned and swam a few yards upstream.

Life flooded back.

So far, I had been hammered round the ring. Miraculously, I had survived that first determined rush. But now it was time I attacked, and stopped fooling about chest deep with my fish a hundred yards downstream. Up by the shingle bank; that was where I wanted him. That was the place to fight it out.

"Come on, fish," I croaked, mouth dry as dust. "You come along with me."

I began to wade slowly back towards the shingle, my rod at right-angles to the river, its butt hard against my side. And the fish came swimming steadily up, gaining on me, so that a belly of line formed behind him and urged him on.

I felt nothing. There was no sign of him. Not a splash, not a ripple. No tugging or pulling. But I knew he was somewhere out there in the darkness; a huge, grey shape, swimming steadily on, his earlier fear replaced by puzzlement at feeling resistance from behind, and now swimming upstream to escape it.

At the top of the shingle I began cautiously to wind in the slack, watching the rapidly changing angle of line against the surface glimmer, careful not to tighten on him too suddenly.

The fish was almost level with me and, although I knew it was still anybody's fight, I sensed the first intimation of success. He had made his great effort, and failed. Now he was going to do what I wanted. I knew there was another rush coming, perhaps more than one, but no rush he made now would equal the first. He was mine – if the hook held.

At last the fish was where I wanted him – above me in the neck of the pool. Now it was time to wake him up and start the second round.

I reeled in and tightened hard on him; tactics that met with instant reaction. Feeling sudden pressure from his flank, the fish tugged and bored, and tugged and turned and twisted and tugged again.

"That's right," I said. "Go on, fish. Fight. Rush about. Do anything – except stay still."

I kept the pressure on, giving him as much stick as I dared. After a minute or two of this he swung suddenly in a wide arc, slashed furiously on the surface, then came straight towards me leaving a huge 'V' shaped ripple on the surface and almost running himself aground. Feeling the stones under his belly he swirled round, shot away again into deep water and started his second rush. Prepared for it, I let him go; the stripped line running out through my fingers.

He went whizzing down to the pool tail, and I followed him to the shingle's end. But this time he turned short of the glide beyond and plunged in the shallows.

"I've got you," I said. "You're nearly done now."

But the tail of a pool is no place for a tired fish.

I walked him steadily upstream again, this time keeping the pressure on, and he followed me like a dog.

At the head of the pool he went deep, boring and twisting. I could feel him down there, shaking his head. I pulled him downstream a few yards and he swung in towards the bank, turning half on his side so that his flank flashed in the brightening moonlight.

Glancing over my shoulder, I saw the moon's edge peeping above the fell. I stepped into the shadow of overhanging trees and stood quite still, the handle of the big salmon net between my knees, the net's rim lying on the bottom in slack water.

The fish was swimming very slowly now, wallowing in small circles. I lifted the rod and it arced against the stars as the fish came in towards me.

The moon rose above the fell and shadows slanted across the pool. Now every stone on the bottom was visible in the clear water and I could see the fish – a long bar of silver just below the surface only a rod's length from me.

I drew him gently in over the sunken net.

I raised the net. It came up six inches – and stuck solid. With a sensation of incredulity and despair I realised it was fastened to something on the bottom. I wrenched at it. It remained immovable, firmly held – as I discovered later – by a piece of barbed-wire jammed between the stones.

Frightened by this commotion, the fish roused himself and rushed away across the pool.

For what seemed eternity he hung doggedly out in the current. I sensed the thrust of his tail against the leader as he stood on his nose boring down among the rocks, and my heart was in my throat.

Sweating, I managed at last to pump him up. He came into the shallows on his side, a swathe of silver in the moonlight.

As he touched the stones, the hook flew from his mouth into the bushes behind me.

For a terrible moment I stood paralysed, while the great fish splashed violently in a cloud of spray. Then, dropping the rod, I plunged in and seized him by the tail. He writhed from my grasp and skidded away towards deeper water. Again, my fingers slipped on his slimy flanks. Now he was nearly able to swim. Almost demented I fell on hands and knees beside him, got both arms underneath and heaved him up on the shingle. He began to flop back towards the river, but I stumbled forward and flung myself on top of him.

* * *

A faint wind whispered in the leaves. The moon had climbed above me and the river was a flashing silver stream that sang in the shallows.

I emptied my waders and sat beneath the sycamore, the great fish gleaming from the grass at my feet. I looked at him in wonder. The biggest sea trout I had ever caught, or was ever likely to catch. The fish of a life-time. He was even bigger than he had seemed when I first saw him. Without doubt he was the same fish: on his right flank just above the anal fin was that round, white lamprey scar.

I sat there for a long time looking at my fish, consumed with fierce elation, and yet – a curious regret. For years, season by season, this fish had survived the long dangerous journey from some distant tide rip to his lonely redds. A miracle of survival.

And now I had caught him.

For years I had fished, night after night the seasons through, dreaming of catching such a fish. And yet now I sat staring at his vast girth, feeling a strange emptiness.

Always, I had wished for the moon and travelled in hope. But now I had arrived . . . and the moon was at my feet.

I threaded a forked stick through his gills and carried him across dew-wet fields up the hill to the cottage. There, I put him on the kitchen table, lighted a lamp, changed my sodden clothes and sat looking out across the valley. Already, a pale oyster light of dawn was spreading above the fells.

Nailed boots sounded in the lane. The labrador jumped growling from his bed beside the stove, then stood wagging his tail in recognition. My fishing companions appeared in the open doorway, stopping with sudden exclamation as they glimpsed what was lying on the table.

They came gingerly inside.

"A *sea trout?*"

"Yes."

"It *can't* be."

"It is. Look at his tail. Count the scales."

They gazed in awe.

"God in heaven! What an incredible fish . . . !"

Darkness lifted from the valley. We sat in the kitchen drinking coffee and whisky while the sky caught fire and the birds sang. Below us the river was a ribbon of mist. Fields beyond the river shone green and yellow in the early sunshine. Curlews were crying from the fells.

My companions debated whether to go to bed or try the sea pool for a whopper come in on the night tide. At length, inspired by whisky and the sight of my fish, they took up their bags and rods and went out again into the clear, cool morning.

Their footsteps faded.

For once I had no desire to accompany them. I thought of my sea trout in the dark sway of the sea, swimming his hours away under the stars – and stayed where I was, feeling no particular pleasure, just a vague regret, an intangible sense of defeat, with the great fish lying there on the table, staring at me with his dead eyes and seeing nothing.

XV
D o g

This little piece is about fishing companionship; but not the companionship of humans, you understand. Life is a chamber of horrors and it was largely to avoid its constantly unfolding tapestry of inhuman nature, that I decided to 'drop out' and live where I do.

Looking back across a lifetime, it comes as no surprise when I consider the solace I have found in the company of my dogs. Oh, there have been and are some notable human exceptions, of course. But for me, canine company at the waterside has generally speaking been so much more congenial. As fishing companions, dogs have one great virtue: they don't chatter.

Mind you, I feel less strongly about it these days. Not because age has made me more tolerant of the human voice; it is simply that as I grow older there is no longer the same urge to catch fish. There is not the same compulsion, the same atavistic drive.

Just as well perhaps, because what with the ravages of netting at sea, excessive poaching, water abstraction, acid rain and other forms of pollution there is not so much left to catch.

It was all very different years ago when the rivers were blue with fish and I spent every spare moment, day and night the seasons through, finding out how to catch them and trying all sorts of new tricks. As any experienced angler knows, success depends largely on attention to detail, which is made possible only by concentration, and you cannot concentrate when people are chattering. At least, I can't. So, in the days when catching fish meant so much to me and when I took those returning shoals of flashing, tide-lice-covered sea trout and salmon for granted; when I wanted to experiment; to think, to try to find out how to induce those non-feeding, unpredictable, creatures to take my fly, I nearly always fished alone.

Of course some people, quite a lot of people, don't like fishing alone, especially for sea trout at night. 'Men fear death,' wrote Bacon, 'as children fear to go in the dark.' But not only children fear the dark. Many a solitary fisherman has funked the long walk home through the eerie, owl-hooting woods, which is not so surprising in this modern age of muggings when poachers arm themselves and work in gangs. For anyone of nervous disposition who finds himself beside a lonely river in the darkening, two people are not twice one; two, quite suddenly, becomes two hundred times one. Nevertheless, despite the hidden dangers of the dark, fishing alone came very naturally to me because, in the absence of well-meaning friends who otherwise would have come along for a chat just when I was trying to concentrate on fishing sunk line in the still watches of the second-half, I enjoyed the silent companionship of my dogs.

The best fishing mate I ever had was my old labrador, Dog. That was his name. Unusual perhaps to call a dog Dog, but there it is. For some reason most of my dogs, a long line of labradors have had idiosyncratic names. There was Jan-Dog, Stinky Wow-Wow, Princeyboy, Diddy, Drakie, Poochie-Poo and Lee-lee, all splendid workers and companions, with Dog at the head of the list – although he was not always in that exalted position.

To start with, Dog would retrieve nothing. He showed an interest in anything that was thrown, but refused to pick it up, let alone bring it back. He seemed un-trainable. After a while I began to think that this time I had picked a wrong 'un.

I remembered the eccentricities of some of the dogs belonging to my friends – one shooting chum in particular, who always took two dogs with him: a labrador and a spaniel. The labrador, contrary to the reputation and origin of its breed, refused to get its feet wet and would retrieve only from land. The spaniel on the other hand, spurned anything that fell on dry land and retrieved only from water. My friend, a keen wildfowler, found the use of both dogs obligatory.

Had I reared a retriever that was totally non-retrieving, either from land or water?

The shooting season, the first I would have expected to use Dog, wound on its way to Christmas with no improvement. On Christmas Eve there were two friends staying at the cottage and we all went out visiting with the banjo, carol singing, until midnight. Well, we started by singing but, what with one thing and another, finished up in something of a heap and were returned by taxi.

The next morning, not feeling too strong, I found my way down to the kitchen to warm my stockings on the Aga. There, on his bed beside the stove, lay Dog; tail wagging, delighted as always to see me. I looked at him with a sense of injustice welling up inside me. What had I done to deserve such an animal? Lovable, indeed, but useless.

After all, to be practical, leaving companionship aside, it costs just as much to cosset and feed a useless dog as it does a useful dog. Surely, I thought, a dog with a pedigree as good as Dog's, must hold some hidden talent somewhere.

"Look," I said, on a sudden idiotic impulse, rolling my stockings up into a ball. "Here's a nice, soft, warm dummy to retrieve. Now, come along, Dog. Fetch." Opening the kitchen door I threw the ball of stockings across the lane, intending to land it beside the dry-stone wall. Over-pitched, it cleared the wall and disappeared into the brackens beyond. Dog bounded across the lane and leaped over the wall. I waited.

"Come on." I shouted after a time. "Fetch it here . . . Good dog. Heel!"

Dutifully, Dog reappeared. Obedient, but empty-mouthed. It was bitterly cold. I was almost naked. But there was nothing for it but to run down to the field gate and retrieve those stockings myself.

Back in the kitchen a feeling of desperation seized me. I would, I determined, make one last effort. Holding the rolled-up pair of stockings in my mouth to show him how it was done, I started to crawl about on the floor on all-fours.

Dog sat in the kitchen armchair watching me intently. Was there a hint of derision in those big amber eyes? If so, it was nothing to the derision of my shooting friends, who had come downstairs in search of headache pills and stomach settlers.

'Well, sod them,' I thought. 'Let them jeer. They know no more about canine psychology than I do.' But my spell of enthusiasm was ended. And so was Dog's last lesson. But, it was not the end of the story.

Far out on the salt marshes, a few mornings later at daybreak, Dog retrieved three wigeon in quick succession, although he had never before held a duck in his mouth. Flighting on a westerly gale, the birds fell among thick sea-blight a couple of hundred yards away downwind, and would have been notable retrieves for any dog, however experienced.

As soon as he returned with the first bird, Dog handed it to me and, unbidden, to my utter astonishment disappeared in quest of the second – which he must have seen me shoot during his absence. And so with the third.

It is said that truth is stranger than fiction. Well, here is an example. I would never have dared to invent such a story. It belongs to the world of pulp magazine fantasy. But it happened just as I have written. Almost overnight, Dog became a fully competent retriever. It was like watching a novice batsman who had never scored a run, go in and make a hundred.

After that wild winter sunrise on the salt marshes just before the New Year, Dog never looked back. Somehow, suddenly, the proverbial penny had well and truly dropped.

I never for one moment believed that Dog's remarkable feat could in any way have been due to my last despairing lesson on Christmas morning in the kitchen. But I pretended I did. And at least it silenced my friends.

In time, Dog became a truly great wildfowler and a superb swimmer. He enjoyed fishing as he enjoyed shooting and his affinity with the river equalled that of the marsh.

Some of my friends extol the virtues of the spaniel, and I have known some beauties, but for me it has always been the labrador. Finest of all companions.

On wild winter afternoons, beside a curve on the river below a reach I used to call 'the Run', Dog and I would wait for duck that came flighting up-river from the estuary. They were mostly mallard, but sometimes there would be flocks of teal and, in very wet weather, when the water meadows were awash, a few wigeon.

The Run was one of my favourite stretches of sea trout night fly fishing – fifty yards or so of streamy water flowing between banks of silver birch and sycamore and alder, leafed-in on top almost like a tunnel. The lower branches were cut back up to rod-top height, so that a fly could pitch within inches of the far bank. It had to, the fish lay right over on that side among the rocks. They took on the first yard or so of the swing. It was roll-casting all the way down in breast waders. You couldn't get out of the water once you started, the bank was too steep and heavily bushed; if you hooked a big chap you played him where you stood. You needed strong terminal tackle and a lot of backing.

At the tail of the Run you could climb ashore where the bank levelled out into a patch of grass I called 'the Square'. Dog would sit on the Square and wait for me. When I landed a fish I would kill it in the net, then throw it up on the bank, and Dog would come along and collect it and carry it back to the Square, and guard it. In those long-ago happy days the river teemed with fish. By the time I had waded down and joined him, Dog would be sitting there, tail wagging, guarding half-a-dozen or more big sea trout all laid out side by side.

Over the years I've heard of fish being lost to otters, mink, pigs, rats, cats, badgers and creeping humans, but it never happened to me when Dog was on duty.

Dog turned out to have a fine nose for game and, in his hey-day, besides fish, would retrieve anything from anywhere. So I really didn't begrudge him his weakness for rabbits. Well, we're none of us perfect. And after all, he wasn't going to compete in any field trials. At the covert-side I anchored him – so what the hell? I think he dreamed about catching rabbits. He would whimper and woof and jerk his legs about as he hunted in his sleep. How could I deny him that small pleasure? He gave me so much.

Besides, secretly I was always hoping that he would catch me a rabbit. A dog-caught animal contains no pellets, and rabbit pie is one of my favourite dishes. For centuries it has been the countryman's traditional and most treasured meal. Not for nothing would the beaters and dog-handlers on big shoots choose rabbit as a gift instead of game. So, whenever Dog indulged his fancy, he had my tacit support – a heresy I concealed from the more conventionally minded of my shooting companions.

As Dog grew older, and slower, and one of his legs became

poorly, the odds against his catching a rabbit lengthened. He would stop after running ten or fifteen yards in pursuit and just stand there, gazing wistfully at that tantalising little white scut disappearing into the gorse. At length he would turn round with a silly grin on his face and come back looking stupid, and roll about and snort.

The nearest he ever came to success was on a sunny afternoon when I was salmon fishing and wading deep down a rocky gorge. Upstream behind me, opposite the spot where the cliff face rose steeply from gorse-covered moorland, there was a sudden splash. It sounded like a jumping fish, but a moment or two later – heading downstream with surprising speed and determination – a rabbit came swimming past. Oddly enough, the little animal didn't swim between me and the cliff, but passed me on the outside – almost as though it had sensed that further out from the bank the current was stronger and would lend it speed.

It must have had a built-in survival kit. With an almighty splash, Dog launched himself off the rocks and came panting down in pursuit. I shouted at him as he swam past, but intent only on the rabbit, gaining rapidly and paying no attention to me whatever, he too chose the outside lane.

Thirty yards downstream the cliff face sloped down again to the open moorland and the rabbit altered course inshore. Dog was close astern now, almost within crunching range, and with the rabbit visibly tiring it seemed that at last Dog would have his day.

But oh dear, no. Foiled again, as they say. Snatching victory from what were literally the jaws of defeat, the rabbit jinked to one side, hopped out of the river and bounded up the bank. Swinging round just too late and back-pedalling frantically, Dog was swirled on down by the current and overshot his landing by several yards. By the time I had fished down to him he had abandoned the hunt. Limping to the water's edge he sat grinning at me with that self-conscious look of unique silliness.

And then the day came (so soon it seemed) when the leg cancer spread and he couldn't run at all. We did our best for him. There were two operations. But they didn't work. After the second, he seemed better for a time. Then very early one morning at daybreak I heard him crying. He was in great pain, and I realised that there was no hope whatever.

At that hour we had no chance of a vet, but to let him lie there suffering was unthinkable. To keep a dog is a great responsibility, and I knew that here, alas, was my moment of reckoning. So I took a spade and went down to the Square at the bottom of the Run and dug a hole. Then I got my gun and a piece of chocolate. He was very fond of chocolate. When he saw the gun his tail twitched with pleasure and he fell silent.

"Come on, Doggie," I said softly. "Let's go and shoot some ducks."

The magic in those well-known words roused him, and he came slowly down with me to the river. When we reached the hole I gave him the chocolate . . . and while he was licking it, I shot him.

I took off the old shooting coat I was wearing and spread it out. It's weird how the mind works when wrenched with emotion. Quite silly sometimes. But I just couldn't bear to think of the earth going into his eyes . . .

So I wrapped him up and covered his head and buried him there in the place where we flighted ducks at winter sunset, and where on bog-myrtle-scented summer nights he would wait for me and guard the fish. And later I painted his name and the date on a big flat stone.

Well, all that happened a long time ago. Since then the letters and the numbers have followed the vanishing runs of fish and been washed away by the weather and many a winter flood. But the stone remains. And when I walk past it, as I sometimes do, I like to think of him lying there beside the river that gave us both so much pleasure.

* * *

You will probably think me very sentimental. And perhaps I am. But I don't care. You see, although times have changed and fishing the Run is only a memory, I can pass the place without regret. I gave that dog as good a life as I could – and when the time came, as quick a death.

I only hope that one day, if necessary, someone will do as much for me.